ONE HUNDRED

FAVOURITE POEMS

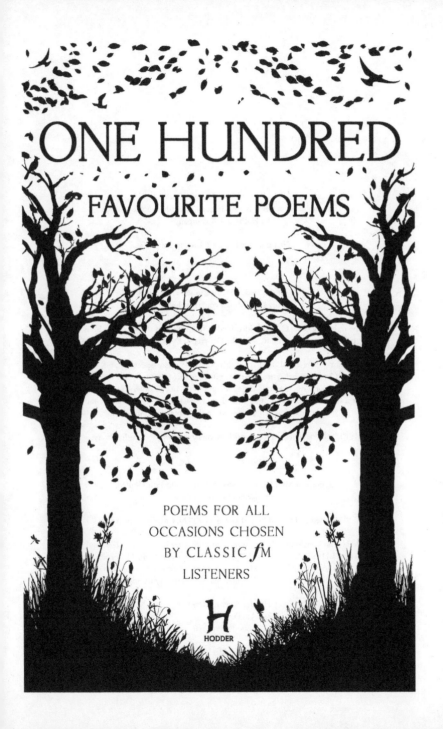

ONE HUNDRED
FAVOURITE POEMS

POEMS FOR ALL
OCCASIONS CHOSEN
BY CLASSIC *f*M
LISTENERS

H
HODDER

First published in Great Britain in 2009 by Hodder & Stoughton
An Hachette UK company

First published in paperback in 2010

14

Copyright © Classic FM 2009 in the arrangement
Poems © individual copyright holders

The right of Classic FM to be identified as the Author of the Work has been
asserted by them in accordance with the Copyright, Designs and Patents Act 1988.

A CIP catalogue record for this title is available from the British Library.

ISBN 978 0 340 92004 6

Typeset in Minion by Palimpsest Book Production Limited,
Grangemouth, Stirlingshire

Printed and bound by CPI Group (UK) Ltd, Croydon, CR0 4YY

Hodder & Stoughton policy is to use papers that are natural, renewable and
recyclable products and made from wood grown in sustainable forests.
The logging and manufacturing processes are expected to conform
to the environmental regulations of the country of origin.

Hodder & Stoughton Ltd
338 Euston Road
London NW1 3BH

www.hodder.co.uk

CONTENTS

Do you remember the first poem you ever heard? It was probably at school. Perhaps, like me, it was 'The Pied Piper'? 'There was a rustling, that seemed like a bustling . . .' – exciting words that immediately conjure up a host of memories. One extraordinary thing is that children have no negative feelings about poetry and will write their own at the drop of a hat. As we get older we seem to be more reserved about reading poetry, which is a terrible shame, because it's a great source of delight and even comfort. Somehow, poetry seems to unlock and express emotions in a way that prose just doesn't. Poems are read at funerals because they express all sorts of feelings that people can't put into their own words. That's what inspired us to include suggestions of poems for various occasions at the end of this book – you'll probably have your own choices to add to these lists.

In many ways poetry is like music. Often we can say that a particular piece of music or a poem has affected us, but we can't say why or how. Just as it's hard to put into words what music like 'The Lark Ascending' by Vaughan Williams does for us, so it is difficult to describe how Edward Thomas's poem 'Adlestrop' seems to conjure up such a feeling of Englishness. It just does. And composers have often been moved to set poetry to music – Schubert's and

Strauss's beautiful songs for example, or Vaughan Williams' setting of A.E. Houseman's 'On Wenlock Edge'.

Ten years ago we published two collections of poetry, *Classic FM One Hundred Favourite Poems* and *Classic FM One Hundred Favourite Humorous Poems*, both of which were a great success. We decided that now was a good time to revisit the project, but this time we should combine the two ideas. Why distinguish between humorous and 'serious' poems? So the titles and first line of every poem in those two books were posted on the Classic FM website and people voted for their favourites – and suggested a few that we hadn't thought to include. (It's interesting to reflect that times have changed so much that when we did the original books we could not have done an on-line poll because so few people were on-line!)

It's my feeling, comparing the lists from ten years ago and now, that we are more conscious of military matters now than we were. Wilfred Owen and Rupert Brooke feature higher in the poll than they did – perhaps a reflection that our armed forces are involved in at least two major conflicts around the world. Does poetry offer a source of comfort in troubled times? The fact that 'If', by Rudyard Kipling, tops the poll by a considerable margin, rather than Wordsworth's 'The Daffodils', makes me wonder whether we're searching for some direction and certainty that's missing from our lives. 'If you can trust yourself when all men doubt you' is a very inspiring thought, as is: 'If we can meet with Triumph and Disaster / And treat those two imposters just the same'. Whatever the reasons, the success of the earlier books and the interest in the new poll confirm poetry's enduring popularity.

Of course you will make your own mind up about which poem is your particular favourite. Whatever you decide, here are one hundred poems, long and short, serious and humorous, which we hope will comfort, inspire – and entertain.

Darren Henley
Managing Director, Classic FM

Note: the poems in this collection are printed in ascending order of popularity, number 100 to number 1. Lists of first lines and titles of poems in alphabetical order may be found at the back of the book.

Sir Henry Newbolt
HE FELL AMONG THIEVES

'Ye have robbed,' said he, 'ye have slaughtered and made an end,
  Take your ill-got plunder, and bury the dead:
What will ye more of your guest and sometime friend?'
  'Blood for our blood,' they said.

He laughed: 'If one may settle the score for five,
  I am ready; but let the reckoning stand till day:
I have loved the sunlight as dearly as any alive.'
  'You shall die at dawn,' said they.

He flung his empty revolver down the slope,
  He climbed alone to the Eastward edge of the trees;
All night long in a dream untroubled of hope
  He brooded, clasping his knees.

He did not hear the monotonous roar that fills
  The ravine where the Yassin river sullenly flows;
He did not see the starlight on the Laspur hills,
  Or the far Afghan snows.

He saw the April noon on his books aglow,
  The wistaria trailing in at the window wide;

He heard his father's voice from the terrace below
    Calling him down to ride.

He saw the gray little church across the park,
    The mounds that hide the loved and honoured dead;
The Norman arch, the chancel softly dark,
    The brasses black and red.

He saw the School Close, sunny and green,
    The runner beside him, the stand by the parapet wall,
The distant tape, and the crowd roaring between
    His own name over all.

He saw the dark wainscot and timbered roof,
    The long tables, and the faces merry and keen;
The College Eight and their trainer dining aloof,
    The Dons on the dais serene.

He watched the liner's stem ploughing the foam,
    He felt her trembling speed and the thrash of her screw;
He heard her passengers' voices talking of home,
    He saw the flag she flew.

And now it was dawn. He rose strong on his feet,
    And strode to his ruined camp below the wood;
He drank the breath of the morning cool and sweet;
    His murderers round him stood.

Light on the Laspur hills was broadening fast,
    The blood-red snow-peaks chilled to a dazzling white:

He turned, and saw the golden circle at last,
   Cut by the Eastern height.

'O glorious Life, Who dwellest in earth and sun,
   I have lived, I praise and adore Thee.'
                              A sword swept.
Over the pass the voices one by one
   Faded, and the hill slept.

99

Harold Monro
OVERHEARD ON A SALT MARSH

Nymph, nymph, what are your beads?
Green glass, goblin. Why do you stare at them?
Give them me.
No.
Give them me. Give them me.
No.
Then I will howl all night in the reeds. Lie in the mud and howl
    for them.
Goblin, why do you love them so?
They are better than stars or water,
Better than voices of winds that sing,
Better than any man's fair daughter,
Your green glass beads on a silver ring.
Hush, I stole them out of the moon.
Give me your beads. I desire them.
No.
I will howl in a deep lagoon for your green glass beads, I love
    them so. Give them me. Give them me.

No.

John Milton
(FROM) PARADISE LOST, BOOK III

Hail, holy light, offspring of Heav'n first-born,
Or of th'Eternal Coeternal beam
May I express thee unblam'd? since God is light,
And never but in unapproached light
Dwelt from Eternitie, dwelt then in thee,
Bright effluence of bright essence increate.
Or hear'st thou rather pure Ethereal stream,
Whose fountain who shall tell? before the Sun,
Before the Heavens thou wert, and at the voice
Of God, as with a Mantle didst invest
The rising world of waters dark and deep,
Won from the void and formless infinite.
Thee I revisit now with bolder wing,
Escap't the Stygian pool, though long detain'd
In that obscure sojourn, while in my flight
Through utter and through middle darkness borne
With other notes than to th'Orphean Lyre
I sung of Chaos and Eternal Night,
Taught by the heavenly Muse to venture down
The dark descent, and up to reascend,
Though hard and rare: thee I revisit safe,
And feel thy sovran vital Lamp; but thou
Revisit'st not these eyes, that rowle in vain

5

To find thy piercing ray, and find no dawn;
So thick a drop serene hath quenched their Orbs,
Or dim suffusion veil'd. Yet not the more
Cease I to wander where the Muses haunt,
Clear Spring, or shadie Grove, or Sunnie Hill,
Smit with the love of sacred song; but chief
Thee Sion and the flowrie Brooks beneath
That wash thy hallow'd feet, and warbling flow,
Nightly I visit: nor sometimes forget
Those other two equal'd with me in Fate,
So were I equal'd with them in renown,
Blind Thamyris and blind Maeonides,
And Tiresias and Phineus, Prophets old.
Then feed on thoughts, that voluntarie move
Harmonious numbers; as the wakeful Bird
Sings darkling, and in shadiest Covert hid
Tunes her nocturnal Note. Thus with the Year
Seasons return; but not to me returns
Day, or the sweet approach of Ev'n or Morn
Or sight of vernal bloom, or Summer's Rose,
Or flocks, or herds, or human face divine;
But cloud instead, and ever-during dark
Surrounds me, from the cheerful waies of men
Cut off, and for the Book of knowledge fair
Presented with a Universal blank
Of Nature's works to mee expung'd and ras'd,
And wisdome at one entrance quite shut out.
So much the rather thou, Celestial light,
Shine inward, and the mind through all her powers
Irradiate; there plant eyes, all mist from thence
Purge and disperse, that I may see and tell
Of things invisible to mortal sight.

97

Roger McGough
MY BUSSEDUCTRESS

She is as beautiful as bustickets
and smells of old cash
drinks Guinness off duty
eats sausage and mash.
But like everyone else
she has her busdreams too
when the peakhour is over
and theres nothing to do.

A fourposter upstairs
a juke-box inside
there are more ways than one
of enjoying a ride.
Velvet curtains on the windows
thick carpets on the floor
roulette under the stairs
a bar by the door.

Three times a day
shed perform a strip-tease
and during the applause
say nicely 'fares please'.
Upstairs she'd reserve

for men of her choice
invite them along
in her best clippie voice.

She knows it sounds silly
what would the police say
but thinks we'd be happier
if she had her way.
There are so many youngmen
shed like to know better
give herself with the change
if only they'd let her.

She is as beautiful as bustickets
and smells of old cash
drinks Guinness off duty
eats sausage and mash.
But she has her busdreams
hot and nervous
my blueserged queen
of the transport service.

Walter de la Mare
SILVER

Slowly, silently, now the moon
Walks the night in her silver shoon;
This way, and that, she peers, and sees
Silver fruit upon silver trees;
One by one the casements catch
Her beams beneath the silvery thatch;
Couched in his kennel, like a log,
With paws of silver sleeps the dog;
From their shadowy cote the white breasts peep
Of doves in a silver-feathered sleep;
A harvest mouse goes scampering by,
With silver claws, and silver eye;
And moveless fish in the water gleam,
By silver reeds in a silver stream.

Edward Lear
THE JUMBLIES

I
They went to sea in a Sieve, they did,
    In a Sieve they went to sea:
In spite of all their friends could say,
On a winter's morn, on a stormy day,
    In a Sieve they went to sea!
And when the Sieve turned round and round,
And every one cried, 'You'll all be drowned!'
They called aloud, 'Our Sieve ain't big,
But we dont care a button! we don't care a fig!
    In a Sieve we'll go to sea!'
        Far and few, far and few,
            Are the lands where the Jumblies live;
            Their heads are green, and their hands are blue,
                And they went to sea in a Sieve.

II
They sailed in a Sieve, they did,
    In a Sieve they sailed so fast,
With only a beautiful pea-green veil
Tied with a riband by way of a sail,
    To a small tobacco-pipe mast;
And every one said, who saw them go,

'O won't they be soon upset, you know!
For the sky is dark, and the voyage is long,
And happen what may, it's extremely wrong
    In a Sieve to sail so fast!'
        Far and few, far and few,
            Are the lands where the Jumblies live;
            Their heads are green, and their hands are blue,
                And they went to sea in a Sieve.

III
The water it soon came in, it did,
    The water it soon came in;
So to keep them dry, they wrapped their feet
In a pinky paper all folded neat,
    And they fastened it down with a pin.
And they passed the night in a crockery-jar,
And each of them said, 'How wise we are!
Though the sky be dark, and the voyage be long,
Yet we never can think we were rash or wrong,
    While round in our Sieve we spin!'
        Far and few, far and few,
            Are the lands where the Jumblies live;
            Their heads are green, and their hands are blue,
                And they went to sea in a Sieve.

IV
And all night long they sailed away;
    And when the sun went down,
They whistled and warbled a moony song
To the echoing sound of a coppery gong,

In the shade of the mountains brown.
'O Timballo! How happy we are,
When we live in a sieve and a crockery-jar,
And all night long in the moonlight pale,
We sail away with a pea-green sail,
    In the shade of the mountains brown!'
        Far and few, far and few,
            Are the lands where the Jumblies live;
            Their heads are green, and their hands are blue,
                And they went to sea in a Sieve.

V

They sailed to the Western Sea, they did,
    To a land all covered with trees,
And they bought an Owl, and a useful Cart,
And a pound of Rice, and a Cranberry Tart,
    And a hive of silvery Bees.
And they bought a Pig, and some green Jack-daws,
And a lovely Monkey with lollipop paws,
And forty bottles of Ring-Bo-Ree,
    And no end of Stilton Cheese.
        Far and few, far and few,
            Are the lands where the Jumblies live;
            Their heads are green, and their hands are blue,
                And they went to sea in a Sieve.

VI

And in twenty years they all came back,
    In twenty years or more,
And every one said, 'How tall they've grown!

For they've been to the Lakes, and the Torrible Zone,
  And the hills of the Chankly Bore';
And they drank their health, and gave them a feast
Of dumplings made of beautiful yeast;
And every one said, 'If we only live,
We too will go to sea in a Sieve,—
  To the hills of the Chankly Bore!'
    Far and few, far and few,
      Are the lands where the Jumblies live;
    Their heads are green, and their hands are blue,
      And they went to sea in a Sieve.

94

Leigh Hunt
JENNY KISSED ME

Jenny kissed me when we met,
Jumping from the chair she sat in.
Time, you thief! who love to get
Sweets into your list, put that in.
Say I'm weary, say I'm sad;
Say that health and wealth have missed me;
Say I'm growing old, but add –
Jenny kissed me!

93

W. E. Henley
INVICTUS

IV
I. M.
R. T. Hamilton Bruce
(1846–1899)

Out of the night that covers me,
　Black as the Pit from pole to pole,
I thank whatever gods may be
　For my unconquerable soul.

In the fell clutch of circumstance
　I have not winced nor cried aloud.
Under the bludgeonings of chance
　My head is bloody, but unbowed.

Beyond this place of wrath and tears
　Looms but the Horror of the shade,
And yet the menace of the years
　Finds, and shall find, me unafraid.

It matters not how strait the gate,
　How charged with punishments the scroll,
I am the master of my fate:
　I am the captain of my soul.

Thomas Hardy
THE DARKLING THRUSH

I leant upon a coppice gate
When Frost was spectre-grey,
And Winter's dregs made desolate
The weakening eye of day.
The tangled bine-stems scored the sky
Like strings of broken lyres,
And all mankind that haunted nigh
Had sought their household fires.

The land's sharp features seemed to be
The Century's corpse outleant,
His crypt the cloudy canopy,
The wind his death-lament.
The ancient pulse of germ and birth
Was shrunken hard and dry,
And every spirit upon earth
Seemed fervourless as I.

At once a voice arose among
The bleak twigs overhead
In a full-hearted evensong
Of joy illimited;
An aged thrush, frail, gaunt, and small,

In blast-beruffled plume,
Had chosen thus to fling his soul
Upon the growing gloom.

So little cause for carolings
Of such ecstatic sound
Was written on terrestrial things
Afar or nigh around,
That I could think there trembled through
His happy good-night air
Some blessed Hope, whereof he knew
And I was unaware.

91

Kenneth Grahame
DUCKS' DITTY

All along the backwater,
Through the rushes tall,
Ducks are a-dabbling,
Up tails all!

Ducks' tails, drakes' tails,
Yellow feet a-quiver,
Yellow bills all out of sight
Busy in the river!

Slushy green undergrowth
Where the roach swim—
Here we keep our larder,
Cool and full and dim.

Every one for what he likes!
We like to be
Heads down, tails up,
Dabbling free!

High in the blue above
Swifts whirl and call—
We are down a-dabbling
Up tails all!

90

Robert Frost
THE ROAD NOT TAKEN

Two roads diverged in a yellow wood,
And sorry I could not travel both
And be one traveller, long I stood
And looked down one as far as I could
To where it bent in the undergrowth;

Then took the other, as just as fair,
And having perhaps the better claim,
Because it was grassy and wanted wear;
Though as for that the passing there
Had worn them really about the same,

And both that morning equally lay
In leaves no step had trodden black.
Oh, I kept the first for another day!
Yet knowing how way leads on to way,
I doubted if I should ever come back.

I shall be telling this with a sigh
Somewhere ages and ages hence:
Two roads diverged in a wood, and I –
I took the one less travelled by,
And that has made all the difference.

89

Edward Fitzgerald
(FROM) THE RUBAIYAT OF OMAR KHAYYAM

Awake! for Morning in the Bowl of Night
Has flung the Stone that puts the Stars to Flight:
    And Lo! the Hunter of the East has caught
The Sultan's Turret in a Noose of Light.

Dreaming when Dawn's Left Hand was in the Sky
I heard a Voice within the Tavern cry,
    'Awake, my Little ones, and fill the Cup
'Before Life's Liquor in its Cup be dry.'

And, as the Cock crew, those who stood before
The Tavern shouted – 'Open then the Door!
    'You know how little while we have to stay,
'And, once departed, may return no more.'

Now the New Year reviving old Desires,
The thoughful Soul to Solitude retires,
    Where the WHITE HAND OF MOSES on the Bough
Puts out, and Jesus from the Ground suspires.

Iram indeed is gone with all its Rose,
And Jamshyd's Sev'n-ring'd Cup where no one knows;
   But still the Vine her ancient Ruby yields,
And still a Garden by the Water blows.

And David's Lips are lock't; but in divine
High-piping Pehlevi, with 'Wine! Wine! Wine!
   'Red Wine!' – the Nightingale cries to the Rose
That yellow Cheek of hers to incarnadine.

Come, fill the Cup, and in the Fire of Spring
The Winter Garment of Repentance fling:
   The Bird of Time has but a little way
To fly – and Lo! the Bird is on the Wing.

And look – a thousand Blossoms with the Day
Woke – and a thousand scatter'd into Clay:
   And this first Summer Month that brings the Rose
Shall take Jamshyd and Kaikobad away.

But come with old Khayyam, and leave the Lot
Of Kaikobad and Kaikhosru forgot:
   Let Rustum lay about him as he will,
Or Hatim Tai cry Supper – heed them not.

With me along some Strip of Herbage strown
That just divides the desert from the sown,
   Where name of Slave and Sultan scarce is known,
And pity Sultan Mahmud on his Throne.

Here with a Loaf of Bread beneath the Bough,
A Flask of Wine, a Book of Verse – and Thou
     Beside me singing in the Wilderness –
And Wilderness is Paradise enow.

'How sweet is mortal Sovranty! think some:
Others – 'How blest the Paradise to come!'
     Ah, take the Cash in hand and waive the Rest;
Oh, the brave Music of a *distant* Drum!

88

T. S. Eliot
THE WASTE LAND

Part I: The Burial of the Dead

April is the cruellest month, breeding
Lilacs out of the dead land, mixing
Memory and desire, stirring
Dull roots with spring rain.
Winter kept us warm, covering
Earth in forgetful snow, feeding
A little life with dried tubers.
Summer surprised us, coming over the Starnbergersee
With a shower of rain; we stopped in the colonnade,
And went on in sunlight, into the Hofgarten,
And drank coffee, and talked for an hour.
Bin gar keine Russin, stamm' aus Litauen, echt deutsch.
And when we were children, staying at the arch-duke's,
My cousin's, he took me out on a sled,
And I was frightened. He said, Marie,
Marie, hold on tight. And down we went.
In the mountains, there you feel free.
I read, much of the night, and go south in the winter.

What are the roots that clutch, what branches grow
Out of this stony rubbish? Son of man,

You cannot say, or guess, for you know only
A heap of broken images, where the sun beats,
And the dead tree gives no shelter, the cricket no relief,
And the dry stone no sound of water. Only
There is shadow under this red rock,
(Come in under the shadow of this red rock),
And I will show you something different from either
Your shadow at morning striding behind you
Or you shadow at evening rising to meet you;
I will show you fear in a handful of dust.

> *Frisch weht der Wind*
> *Der Heimat zu*
> *Mein Irisch Kind*
> *Wo weilest du?*

'You gave me hyacinths first a year ago;
'They called me the hyacinth girl.'
– Yet when we came back, late, from the hyacinth garden,
Your arms were full, and your hair wet, I could not
Speak, and my eyes failed, I was neither
Living nor dead, and I knew nothing,
Looking into the heart of light, the silence.
Oed' und leer das Meer.

Madame Sosostris, famous clairvoyante,
Had a bad cold, nevertheless
Is known to be the wisest woman in Europe,
With a wicked pack of cards. Here, said she,
Is your card, the drowned Phoenician Sailor,
(Those are pearls that were his eyes. Look!)
Here is Belladonna, the Lady of the Rocks,

The lady of situations,
Here is the man with three staves, and here the Wheel,
And here is the one-eyed merchant, and this card,
Which is blank, is something he carries on his back,
Which I am forbidden to see. I do not find
The Hanged Man. Fear death by water.
I see crowds of people, walking round in a ring.
Thank you. If you see dear Mrs Equitone,
Tell her I bring the horoscope myself:
One must be so careful these days.

    Unreal City,
Under the brown fog of a winter dawn,
A crowd flowed over London Bridge, so many,
I had not thought death had undone so many.
Sighs, short and infrequent, were exhaled,
And each man fixed his eyes before his feet.
Flowed up the hill and down King William Street,
To where Saint Mary Woolnoth kept the hours
With a dead sound on the final stroke of nine.
There I saw one I knew, and stopped him, crying: 'Stetson!
'You who were with me in the ships at Mylae!
'That corpse you planted last year in your garden,
'Has it begun to sprout? Will it bloom this year?
'Or has the sudden frost disturbed its bed?
'O keep the Dog far hence, that's friend to men,
'Or with his nails he'll dig it up again!
'You! hypocrite lecteur! – mon semblable, – mon frère!'

G. K. Chesterton
(FROM) LEPANTO

White founts falling in the courts of the sun,
And the Soldan of Byzantium is smiling as they run;
There is laughter like the fountains in that face of all men
    feared,
It stirs the forest darkness, the darkness of his beard,
It curls the blood-red crescent, the crescent of his lips,
For the inmost sea of all the earth is shaken with his ships.
They have dared the white republics up the capes of Italy,
They have dashed the Adriatic round the Lion of the Sea,
And the Pope has cast his arms abroad for agony and loss,
And called the kings of Christendom for swords about the
    Cross,
The cold queen of England is looking in the glass;
The shadow of the Valois is yawning at the Mass;
From evening isles fantastical rings faint the Spanish gun,
And the Lord upon the Golden Horn is laughing in the sun.

Dim drums throbbing, in the hills half heard,
Where only on a nameless throne a crownless prince has stirred,
Where, risen from a doubtful seat and half-attainted stall,
The last knight of Europe takes weapons from the wall,
The last and lingering troubadour to whom the bird has sung,
That once went singing southward when all the world was young,

In that enormous silence, tiny and unafraid,
Comes up along a winding road the noise of the Crusade.
Strong gongs groaning as the guns boom far,
Don John of Austria is going to the war,
Stiff flags straining in the night-blasts cold
In the gloom black-purple, in the glint old-gold,
Torchlight crimson on the copper kettle-drums,
Then the tuckets, then the trumpets, then the cannon, and he
  comes.
Don John laughing in the brave beard curled,
Spurning of his stirrups like the thrones of all the world,
Holding his head up for a flag of all the free.
Love-light of Spain – hurrah!
Death-light of Africa!
Don John of Austria
Is riding to the sea.

Robert Browning
(FROM) THE PIED PIPER

There was a rustling, that seemed like a bustling
Of merry crowds justling at pitching and hustling,
Small feet were pattering, wooden shoes clattering,
Little hands clapping and little tongues chattering,
And, like fowls in a farmyard when barley is scattering,
Out came the children running.
All the little boys and girls,
With rosy cheeks and flaxen curls,
And sparkling eyes and teeth like pearls,
Tripping and skipping, ran merrily after
The wonderful music with shouting and laughter.

The Mayor was dumb, and the Council stood
As if they were changed into blocks of wood,
Unable to move a step, or cry
To the children merrily skipping by
– Could only follow with the eye
That joyous crowd at the Piper's back.
But how the Mayor was on the rack,
And the wretched Council's bosoms beat,
As the Piper turned from the High Street
To where the Weser rolled its waters
Right in the way of their sons and daughters!

However he turned from south to west,
And to Koppelberg Hill his steps addressed,
And after him the children pressed;
Great was the joy in every breast.
'He never can cross that mighty top!
He's forced to let the piping drop,
And we shall see our children stop!'
When, lo, as they reached the mountain-side,
A wondrous portal opened wide,
As if a cavern was suddenly hollowed;
And the Piper advanced and the children followed,
And when all were in to the very last,
The door in the mountain-side shut fast.
Did I say, all? No! One was lame,
    And could not dance the whole of the way;
And in after years, if you would blame
    His sadness, he was used to say –
'It's dull in our town since my playmates left!
I can't forget that I'm bereft
Of all the pleasant sights they see
Which the Piper also promised me.
For he led us, he said, to a joyous land,
Joining the town and just at hand
Where waters gushed and fruit trees grew
And flowers put forth a fairer hue,
And everything was strange and new;
The sparrows were brighter than peacocks here,
And their dogs outran our fallow deer,
And honey-bees had lost their stings,
And horses were born with eagles' wings:

And just as I became assured
My lame foot would be speedily cured,
The music stopped and I stood still,
And found myself outside the hill,
Left alone against my will,
To go now limping as before,
And never hear of that country more!'

85

William Blake
AUGURIES OF INNOCENCE

To see a world in a grain of sand,
And a heaven in a wild flower,
Hold infinity in the palm of your hand,
And eternity in an hour.

A robin redbreast in a cage
Puts all heaven in a rage.

A dove-house fill'd with doves and pigeons
Shudders hell thro' all its regions.
A dog starv'd at his master's gate
Predicts the ruin of the state.

A horse misused upon the road
Calls to heaven for human blood.
Each outcry of the hunted hare
A fibre from the brain does tear.

A skylark wounded in the wing,
A cherubim does cease to sing.
The game-cock clipt and arm'd for fight
Does the rising sun affright.

Every wolf's and lion's howl
Raises from hell a human soul.

The wild deer, wand'ring here and there,
Keeps the human soul from care.
The lamb misus'd breeds public strife,
And yet forgives the butcher's knife.

The bat that flits at close of eve
Has left the brain that won't believe.
The owl that calls upon the night
Speaks the unbeliever's fright.

He who shall hurt the little wren
Shall never be belov'd by men.
He who the ox to wrath has mov'd
Shall never be by woman lov'd.

The wanton boy that kills the fly
Shall feel the spider's enmity.
He who torments the chafer's sprite
Weaves a bower in endless night.

The caterpillar on the leaf
Repeats to thee thy mother's grief.
Kill not the moth nor butterfly,
For the last judgement draweth nigh.

He who shall train the horse to war
Shall never pass the polar bar.

32

The beggar's dog and widow's cat,
Feed them and thou wilt grow fat.

The gnat that sings his summer's song
Poison gets from slander's tongue.
The poison of the snake and newt
Is the sweat of envy's foot.

The poison of the honey bee
Is the artist's jealousy.

The prince's robes and beggar's rags
Are toadstools on the miser's bags.
A truth that's told with bad intent
Beats all the lies you can invent.

It is right it should be so;
Man was made for joy and woe;
And when this we rightly know,
Thro' the world we safely go.

Joy and woe are woven fine,
A clothing for the soul divine.
Under every grief and pine
Runs a joy with silken twine.

The babe is more than swaddling bands;
Throughout all these human lands
Tools were made and born were hands
Every farmer understands.

Every tear from every eye
Becomes a babe in eternity.

This is caught by females bright,
And return'd to its own delight.
The bleat, the bark, bellow, and roar,
Are waves that beat on heaven's shore.

The babe that weeps the rod beneath
Writes revenge in realms of death.
The beggar's rags, fluttering in air,
Does to rags the heavens tear.

The soldier, arm'd with sword and gun,
Palsied strikes the summer's sun.
The poor man's farthing is worth more
Than all the gold on Afric's shore.

One mite wrung from the lab'rer's hands
Shall buy and sell the miser's lands;
Or, if protected from on high,
Does that whole nation sell and buy.

He who mocks the infant's faith
Shall be mock'd in age and death.
He who shall teach the child to doubt
The rotting grave shall ne'er get out.

He who respects the infant's faith
Triumphs over hell and death.

The child's toys and the old man's reasons
Are the fruits of the two seasons.

The questioner, who sits so sly,
Shall never know how to reply.
He who replies to words of doubt
Doth put the light of knowledge out.

The strongest poison ever known
Came from Caesar's laurel crown.
Nought can deform the human race
Like to the armour's iron brace.

When gold and gems adorn the plow,
To peaceful arts shall envy bow.
A riddle, or the cricket's cry,
Is to doubt a fit reply.

The emmet's inch and eagle's mile
Make lame philosophy to smile.
He who doubts from what he sees
Will ne'er believe, do what you please.

If the sun and moon should doubt,
They'd immediately go out.
To be in a passion you good may do,
But no good if a passion is in you.

The whore and gambler, by the state
Licensed, build that nation's fate.

The harlot's cry from street to street
Shall weave old England's winding-sheet.

The winner's shout, the loser's curse,
Dance before dead England's hearse.

Every night and every morn
Some to misery are born,
Every morn and every night
Some are born to sweet delight.

Some are born to sweet delight,
Some are born to endless night.

We are led to believe a lie
When we see not thro' the eye,
Which was born in a night to perish in a night,
When the soul slept in beams of light.

God appears, and God is light,
To those poor souls who dwell in night;
But does a human form display
To those who dwell in realms of day.

84

W. H. Auden
NIGHT MAIL

I
This is the Night Mail crossing the Border,
Bringing the cheque and the postal order,

Letters for the rich, letters for the poor,
The shop at the corner, the girl next door.

Pulling up Beattock, a steady climb:
The gradient's against her, but she's on time.

Past cotton-grass and moorland boulder,
Shovelling white steam over her shoulder,

Snorting noisily, she passes
Silent miles of wind-bent grasses.

Birds turn their heads as she approaches,
Stare from bushes at her blank-faced coaches.

Sheep-dogs cannot turn her course;
They slumber on with paws across.

In the farm she passes no one wakes,
But a jug in a bedroom gently shakes.

II
Dawn freshens. Her climb is done.
Down towards Glasgow she descends,
Towards the steam tugs yelping down a glade of cranes,
Towards the fields of apparatus, the furnaces
Set on the dark plain like gigantic chessmen.
All Scotland waits for her:
In dark glens, beside pale-green lochs,
Men long for news.

III
Letters of thanks, letters from banks,
Letters of joy from girl and boy,
Receipted bills and invitations
To inspect new stock or to visit relations,
And applications for situations,
And timid lovers' declarations,
And gossip, gossip from all the nations,
News circumstantial, news financial,
Letters with holiday snaps to enlarge in,
Letters with faces scrawled on the margin,
Letters from uncles, cousins and aunts,
Letters to Scotland from the South of France,
Letters of condolence to Highlands and Lowlands,
Written on paper of every hue,
The pink, the violet, the white and the blue,
The chatty, the catty, the boring, the adoring,

The cold and official and the heart's outpouring,
Clever, stupid, short and long,
The typed and the printed and the spelt all wrong.

IV
Thousands are still asleep,
Dreaming of terrifying monsters
Or a friendly tea beside the band in Cranston's or Crawford's:
Asleep in working Glasgow, asleep in well-set Edinburgh,
Asleep in granite Aberdeen,
They continue their dreams,
But shall wake soon and hope for letters,
And none will hear the postman's knock
Without a quickening of the heart.
For who can bear to feel himself forgotten?

83

Matthew Arnold
DOVER BEACH

The sea is calm to-night.
The tide is full, the moon lies fair
Upon the Straits; – on the French coast, the light
Gleams, and is gone; the cliffs of England stand,
Glimmering and vast, out in the tranquil bay.
Come to the window, sweet is the night air!
Only, from the long line of spray
Where the ebb meets the moon-blanch'd sand,
Listen! you hear the grating roar
Of pebbles which the waves suck back, and fling,
At their return, up the high strand,
Begin, and cease, and then again begin,
With tremulous cadence slow, and bring
The eternal note of sadness in.

   Sophocles long ago
Heard it on the Aegean, and it brought
Into his mind the turbid ebb and flow
Of human misery; we
Find also in the sound a thought,
Hearing it by this distant northern sea.

The sea of faith
Was once, too, at the full, and round earth's shore
Lay like the folds of a bright girdle furl'd;
But now I only hear
Its melancholy, long, withdrawing roar,
Retreating to the breath
Of the night-wind down the vast edges drear
And naked shingles of the world.

Ah, love, let us be true
To one another! for the world, which seems
To lie before us like a land of dreams,
So various, so beautiful, so new,
Hath really neither joy, nor love, nor light,
Nor certitude, nor peace, nor help for pain;
And we are here as on a darkling plain
Swept with confused alarms of struggle and flight,
Where ignorant armies clash by night.

82

William Wordsworth
THE LOST LOVE

She dwelt among the untrodden ways
  Beside the springs of Dove,
A maid whom there were none to praise,
  And very few to love.

A violet by a mossy stone
  Half-hidden from the eye!—
Fair as a star, when only one
  Is shining in the sky.

She lived unknown, and few could know
  When Lucy ceased to be;
But she is in her grave, and, oh,
  The difference to me!

81

Alfred, Lord Tennyson
THE CHARGE OF THE LIGHT BRIGADE

I
Half a league, half a league,
  Half a league onward,
All in the valley of Death
  Rode the six hundred.
'Forward, the Light Brigade!
Charge for the guns!' he said;
Into the valley of Death
  Rode the six hundred.

II
'Forward, the Light Brigade!'
Was there a man dismay'd?
Not tho' the soldier knew
  Some one had blunder'd:
Their's not to make reply,
Their's not to reason why,
Their's but to do and die:
Into the valley of Death
  Rode the six hundred.

III

Cannon to right of them,
Cannon to left of them,
Cannon in front of them
    Volley'd and thunder'd;
Storm'd at with shot and shell,
Boldly they rode and well,
Into the jaws of Death,
Into the mouth of Hell
    Rode the six hundred.

IV

Flash'd all their sabres bare,
Flash'd as they turn'd in air,
Sabring the gunners there,
Charging an army, while
    All the world wonder'd:
Plunged in the battery-smoke
Right thro' the line they broke;
Cossack and Russian
Reel'd from the sabre-stroke
    Shatter'd and sunder'd.
Then they rode back, but not,
    Not the six hundred.

V

Cannon to right of them,
Cannon to left of them,
Cannon behind them
    Volley'd and thunder'd;

Storm'd at with shot and shell,
While horse and hero fell,
They that had fought so well
Came thro' the jaws of Death
Back from the mouth of Hell,
All that was left of them,
  Left of six hundred.

VI
When can their glory fade?
O the wild charge they made!
  All the world wonder'd.
Honour the charge they made!
Honour the Light Brigade,
  Noble six hundred!

80

Christina Rossetti
REMEMBER

Remember me when I am gone away,
Gone far away into the silent land;
When you can no more hold me by the hand,
Nor I half turn to go yet turning stay.
Remember me when no more day by day
You tell me of our future that you planned:
Only remember me; you understand
It will be late to counsel then or pray.
Yet if you should forget me for a while
And afterwards remember, do not grieve:
For if the darkness and corruption leave
A vestige of the thoughts that once I had,
Better by far you should forget and smile
Than that you should remember and be sad.

79

Christina Rossetti
BY WAY OF REMEMBRANCE

Remember, if I claim too much of you,
I claim it of my brother and my friend:
Have patience with me till the hidden end,
Bitter or sweet, in mercy shut from view.
Pay me my due; though I to pay your due
Am all too poor and past what will can mend:
Thus of your bounty you must give and lend
Still unrepaid by aught I look to do.
Still unrepaid by aught of mine on earth:
But overpaid, please God, when recompense
Beyond the mystic Jordan and new birth
Is dealt to virtue as to innocence;
When Angels singing praises in their mirth
Have borne you in their arms and fetched you hence.

William McGonagall
THE RAILWAY BRIDGE OF THE SILVERY TAY

Beautiful Railway bridge of the Silvery Tay!
With your numerous arches and pillars in so grand array,
And your central girders, which seem to the eye
To be almost towering to the sky.
The greatest wonder of the day,
And a great beautification to the River Tay,
Most beautiful to be seen,
Near by Dundee and the Magdalen Green.

Beautiful Railway Bridge of the Silvery Tay!
That has caused the Emperor of Brazil to leave
His home far away, *incognito* in his dress,
And view thee ere he passed along *en route* to Inverness.

Beautiful Railway Bridge of the Silvery Tay!
The longest of the present day
That has ever crossed o'er a tidal river stream,
Most gigantic to be seen,
Near by Dundee and the Magdalen Green.

Beautiful Railway Bridge of the Silvery Tay!
Which will cause great rejoicing on the opening day,
And hundreds of people will come from far away,

Also the Queen, most gorgeous to be seen,
Near by Dundee and the Magdalen Green.

Beautiful Railway Bridge of the Silvery Tay!
And prosperity to Provost Cox, who has given
Thirty thousand pounds and upwards away
In helping to erect the Bridge of the Tay,
Most handsome to be seen,
Near by Dundee and the Magdalen Green.

Beautiful Railway Bridge of the Silvery Tay!
I hope that God will protect all passengers
By night and by day,
And that no accident will befall them while crossing
The Bridge of the Silvery Tay,
For that would be most awful to be seen
Near by Dundee and the Magdalen Green.

Beautiful Railway Bridge of the Silvery Tay!
And prosperity to Messrs Bouche and Grothe,
The famous engineers of the present day,
Who have succeeded in erecting the Railway
Bridge of the Silvery Tay,
Which stands unequalled to be seen
Near by Dundee and the Magdalen Green.

Henry Wadsworth Longfellow
(FROM) THE SONG OF HIAWATHA

   She had sent through all the village
Messengers with wands of willow,
As a sign of invitation,
As a token of the feasting;
And the wedding-guests assembled,
Clad in all their richest raiment,
Robes of fur and belts of wampum,
Splendid with their paint and plumage,
Beautiful with beads and tassels.
. . .

   He was dressed in shirt of doeskin,
White and soft and fringed with ermine,
All inwrought with beads of wampum;
. . .

On his head were plumes of swan's down,
On his heels were tails of foxes,
In one hand a fan of feathers,
And a pipe was in the other.
. . .

Looking still at Hiawatha,
Looking at fair Laughing Water,
Sang he softly, sang in this wise:
   'Onaway! Awake, beloved!

Thou the wild-flower of the forest!
Thou the wild-bird of the prairie!
Thou with eyes so soft and fawn-like!
   'If thou only lookest at me,
I am happy, I am happy,
As the lilies of the prairie,
When they feel the dew upon them!
   'Sweet thy breath is as the fragrance
Of the wild-flowers in the morning,
As their fragrance is at evening,
In the Moon when leaves are falling.'
. . .
'True is all Iagoo tells us;
I have seen it in a vision,
Seen the great canoe with pinions,
Seen the people with white faces,
Seen the coming of this bearded
People of the wooden vessel
From the regions of the morning,
From the shining land of Wabun.
. . .
   I beheld, too, in that vision
All the secrets of the future,
Of the distant days that shall be.
I beheld the westward marches
Of the unknown, crowded nations.
All the land was full of people,
Restless, struggling, toiling, striving,
Speaking many tongues, yet feeling
But one heart-beat in their bosoms.
In the woodlands rang their axes,

Smoked their towns in all the valleys,
Over all the lakes and rivers
Rushed their great canoes of thunder.
Then a darker, drearier vision
Passed before me, vague and cloud-like.
I beheld our nations scattered,
All forgetful of my counsels,
Weakened, warring with each other;
Saw the remnants of our people
Sweeping westward, wild and woeful,
Like the cloud-rack of a tempest,
Like the withered leaves of autumn!'
. . .

  On the shore stood Hiawatha,
Turned and waved his hand at parting;
On the clear and luminous water
Launched his birch-canoe for sailing,
From the pebbles of the margin
Shoved it forth into the water;
Whispered to it: 'Westward! westward!'
And with speed it darted forward.
  And the evening sun descending
Set the clouds on fire with redness,
Burned the broad sky, like a prairie,
Left upon the level water
One long track and trail of splendour,
Down whose stream, as down a river,
Westward, westward Hiawatha
Sailed into the fiery sunset,
Sailed into the purple vapours,
Sailed into the dusk of evening.

George Herbert
LOVE

Love bade me welcome, yet my soul drew back,
    Guilty of dust and sin.
But quick-eyed Love, observing me grow slack
    From my first entrance in,
Drew nearer to me, sweetly questioning
    If I lacked any thing.

'A guest,' I answer'd, 'worthy to be here';
    Love said, 'You shall be he.'
'I, the unkind, ungrateful? Ah, my dear,
    I cannot look on thee.'
Love took my hand and smiling did reply,
    'Who made the eyes but I?'

'Truth, Lord, but I have marred them; let my shame
    Go where it doth deserve.'
'And know you not,' says Love, 'who bore the blame?'
    'My dear, then I will serve.'
'You must sit down,' says Love, 'and taste my meat.'
    So I did sit and eat.

T. S. Eliot
JOURNEY OF THE MAGI

'A cold coming we had of it.
Just the worst time of the year
For a journey, and such a long journey:
The ways deep and the weather sharp,
The very dead of winter.'
And the camels galled, sore-footed, refractory,
Lying down in the melting snow.
There were times we regretted
The summer palaces on slopes, the terraces.
And the silken girls bringing sherbet.
Then the camel men cursing and grumbling
And running away, and wanting their liquor and women,
And the night-fires going out, and the lack of shelters,
And the cities hostile and the towns unfriendly
And the villages dirty and charging high prices:
A hard time we had of it.
At the end we preferred to travel all night,
Sleeping in snatches,
With the voices singing in our ears, saying
That this was all folly.

Then at dawn we came down to a temperate valley,
Wet, below the snow line, smelling of vegetation,

With a running stream and a water-mill beating the darkness,
And three trees on the low sky.
And an old white horse galloped away in the meadow.
Then we came to a tavern with vine-leaves over the lintel,
Six hands at an open door dicing for pieces of silver,
And feet kicking the empty wine-skins.
But there was no information, and so we continued
And arrived at evening, not a moment too soon
Finding the place; it was (you may say) satisfactory.

All this was a long time ago, I remember,
And I would do it again, but set down
This set down
This: were we led all that way for
Birth or Death? There was a Birth, certainly,
We had evidence and no doubt. I had seen birth and death,
But had thought they were different; this Birth was
Hard and bitter agony for us, like Death, our death.
We returned to our places, these Kingdoms,
But no longer at ease here, in the old dispensation,
With an alien people clutching their gods.
I should be glad of another death.

74

Emily Dickinson
HE FUMBLES AT YOUR SPIRIT

He fumbles at your spirit
  As players at the keys
Before they drop full music on;
  He stuns you by degrees,

Prepares your brittle substance
  For the ethereal blow,
By fainter hammers, further heard,
  Then nearer, then so slow

Your breath has time to straighten,
  Your brain to bubble cool,—
Deals one imperial thunderbolt
  That scalps your naked soul.

73

W. H. Davies
LEISURE

What is this life if, full of care,
We have no time to stand and stare?

No time to stand beneath the boughs
And stare as long as sheep or cows.

No time to see, when woods we pass,
Where squirrels hide their nuts in grass.

No time to see, in broad daylight,
Streams full of stars, like skies at night.

No time to turn at Beauty's glance,
And watch her feet, how they can dance.

No time to wait till her mouth can
Enrich that smile her eyes began.

A poor life this if, full of care,
We have no time to stand and stare.

G. K. Chesterton

THE ROLLING ENGLISH ROAD

Before the Roman came to Rye or out to Severn strode,
The rolling English drunkard made the rolling English road.
A reeling road, a rolling road, that rambles round the shire,
And after him the parson ran, the sexton and the squire;
A merry road, a mazy road, and such as we did tread
That night we went to Birmingham by way of Beachy Head.

I knew no harm of Bonaparte and plenty of the Squire,
And for to fight the Frenchmen I did not much desire;
But I did bash their baggonets because they came arrayed
To straighten out the crooked road an English drunkard made,
Where you and I went down the lane with ale-mugs in our
    hands,
The night we went to Glastonbury by way of Goodwin Sands.

His sins they were forgiven him; or why do flowers run
Behind him; and the hedges all strengthening in the sun?
The wild thing went from left to right and knew not which was
    which
But the wild rose was above him when they found him in the
    ditch
God pardon us, nor harden us; we did not see so clear
The night we went to Bannockburn by way of Brighton Pier.

My friends, we will not go again or ape an ancient rage,
Or stretch the folly of our youth to be the shame of age,
But walk with clearer eyes and ears this path that wandereth,
And see undrugged in evening light the decent inn of death;
For there is good news yet to hear and fine things to be seen,
Before we go to Paradise by way of Kensal Green.

Lewis Carroll
FATHER WILLIAM

'You are old, Father William,' the young man said,
  'And your hair has become very white;
And yet you incessantly stand on your head—
  Do you think, at your age, it is right?'

'In my youth,' Father William replied to his son,
  'I feared it might injure the brain;
But, now that I'm perfectly sure I have none,
  Why, I do it again and again.'

'You are old,' said the youth, 'as I mentioned before,
  And have grown most uncommonly fat;
Yet you turned a back-somersault in at the door—
  Pray, what is the reason of that?'

'In my youth,' said the sage, as he shook his grey locks,
  'I kept all my limbs very supple
By the use of this ointment – one shilling the box—
  Allow me to sell you a couple?'

'You are old,' said the youth, and your jaws are too weak
  For anything tougher than suet;
Yet you finished the goose, with the bones and the beak—
  Pray, how did you manage to do it?'

'In my youth,' said his father, 'I took to the law,
    And argued each case with my wife;
And the muscular strength, which it gave to my jaw,
    Has lasted the rest of my life.'

'You are old,' said the youth, 'one would hardly suppose
    That your eye was as steady as ever;
Yet you balanced an eel on the end of your nose—
    What made you so awfully clever?'

'I have answered three questions, and that is enough,'
    Said his father; dont give yourself airs!
Do you think I can listen all day to such stuff?
    Be off, or I'll kick you down stairs!'

70

Anonymous
DO NOT STAND AT MY GRAVE AND WEEP

Do not stand at my grave and weep;
I am not there. I do not sleep.
I am a thousand winds that blow.
I am the diamond glints on snow.
I am the sunlight on ripened grain.
I am the gentle autumn rain.
When you awaken in the morning's hush
I am the swift uplifting rush
Of quiet birds in circled flight.
I am the soft stars that shine at night.
Do not stand at my grave and cry;
I am not there. I did not die.

69

Anonymous
GREENSLEEVES

Alas, my love, you do me wrong,
To cast me off discourteously.
And I have loved you so long,
Delighting in your company.

Chorus:
Greensleeves was all my joy
Greensleeves was my delight,
Greensleeves was my heart of gold,
And who but my Lady Greensleeves.

Your vows you've broken, like my heart,
Oh, why did you so enrapture me?
Now I remain in a world apart
But my heart remains in captivity.

Chorus

I have been ready at your hand,
To grant whatever you would crave,
I have both wagered life and land,
Your love and good-will for to have.

Chorus

If you intend thus to disdain,
It does the more enrapture me,
And even so, I still remain
A lover in captivity.

Chorus

My men were clothed all in green,
And they did ever wait on thee;
All this was gallant to be seen,
And yet thou wouldst not love me.

Chorus

Thou couldst desire no earthly thing,
but still thou hadst it readily.
Thy music still to play and sing;
And yet thou wouldst not love me.

Chorus

Well, I will pray to God on high,
that thou my constancy mayst see,
And that yet once before I die,
Thou wilt vouchsafe to love me.

Chorus

Ah, Greensleeves, now farewell, adieu,
To God I pray to prosper thee,
For I am still thy lover true,
Come once again and love me.

68

John Masefield
CARGOES

Quinquireme of Nineveh from distant Ophir
Rowing home to haven in sunny Palestine,
With a cargo of ivory,
And apes and peacocks,
Sandalwood, cedarwood, and sweet white wine.

Stately Spanish galleon coming from the Isthmus,
Dipping through the Tropics by the palm-green shores,
With a cargo of diamonds,
Emeralds, amethysts,
Topazes, and cinnamon, and gold moidores.

Dirty British coaster with a salt-caked smoke-stack
Butting through the Channel in the mad March days,
With a cargo of Tyne coal,
Road-rail, pig-lead,
Firewood, iron-ware, and cheap tin trays.

John Masefield
SEA FEVER

I must down to the seas again, to the lonely sea and the sky,
And all I ask is a tall ship and a star to steer her by,
And the wheel's kick and the wind's song and the white sail's
    shaking,
And a grey mist on the sea's face and a grey dawn breaking.

I must down to the seas again, for the call of the running tide
Is a wild call and a clear call that may not be denied;
And all I ask is a windy day with the white clouds flying,
And the flung spray and the blown spume, and the sea-gulls
    crying.

I must down to the seas again, to the vagrant gypsy life,
To the gull's way and the whale's way where the wind's like a
    whetted knife;
And all I ask is a merry yarn from a laughing fellow-rover,
And quiet sleep and a sweet dream when the long trick's over.

D. H. Lawrence
SNAKE

A snake came to my water-trough
On a hot, hot day, and I in pyjamas for the heat,
To drink there.

In the deep, strange-scented shade of the great dark carob-tree
I came down the steps with my pitcher
And must wait, must stand and wait, for there he was at the
    trough before me.

He reached down from a fissure in the earth-wall in the gloom
And trailed his yellow-brown slackness soft-bellied down, over
    the edge of the stone trough
And rested his throat upon the stone bottom,
And where the water had dripped from the tap, in a small
    clearness,
He sipped with his straight mouth,
Softly drank through his straight gums, into his slack long body,
Silently.

Someone was before me at my water-trough,
And I, like a second comer, waiting.

He lifted his head from his drinking, as cattle do,
And looked at me vaguely, as drinking cattle do,
And flickered his two-forked tongue from his lips, and mused a
    moment,
And stooped and drank a little more,
Being earth-brown, earth-golden from the burning bowels of the
    earth
On the day of Sicilian July, with Etna smoking.

The voice of my education said to me
He must be killed,
For in Sicily the black, black snakes are innocent, the gold are
    venomous.

And voices in me said, If you were a man
You would take a stick and break him now, and finish him off.

But must I confess how I liked him,
How glad I was he had come like a guest in quiet, to drink at
    my water-trough
And depart peaceful, pacified, and thankless,
Into the burning bowels of this earth?

Was it cowardice, that I dared not kill him?
Was it perversity, that I longed to talk to him?
Was it humility, to feel so honoured?
I felt so honoured.

And yet those voices:
If you were not afraid, you would kill him!

And truly I was afraid, I was most afraid,
But even so, honoured still more
That he should seek my hospitality
From out the dark door of the secret earth.

He drank enough
And lifted his head, dreamily, as one who has drunken,
And flickered his tongue like a forked night on the air, so black,
Seeming to lick his lips,
And looked around like a god, unseeing, into the air,
And slowly turned his head.
And slowly, very slowly, as if thrice adream,
Proceeded to draw his slow length curving round
And climb again the broken bank of my wall-face.
And as he put his head into that dreadful hole,
And as he slowly drew up, snake-easing his shoulders, and
    entered farther,
A sort of horror, a sort of protest against his withdrawing into
    that horrid black hole,
Deliberately going into the blackness, and slowly drawing
    himself after,
Overcame me now his back was turned.

I looked round, I put down my pitcher,
I picked up a clumsy log
And threw it at the water-trough with a clatter.

I did not think it hit him,
But suddenly that part of him that was left behind convulsed in
    undignified haste,

70

Writhed like lightning, and was gone
Into the black hole, the earth-lipped fissure in the wall-front,
At which, in the intense still noon, I stared with fascination.

And immediately I regretted it.
I thought how paltry, how vulgar, what a mean act!
I despised myself and the voices of my accursed human
    education.

And I thought of the albatross,
And I wished he would come back, my snake.

For he seemed to me again like a king,
Like a king in exile, uncrowned in the underworld,
Now due to be crowned again.

And so, I missed my chance with one of the lords
Of life.
And I have something to expiate;
A pettiness.

Robert Herrick
TO DAFFODILS

Fair Daffodils, we weep to see
   You haste away so soon;
As yet the early rising sun
   Has not attained his noon.
      Stay, stay,
   Until the hasting day
      Has run
   But to the evensong,
And, having prayed together, we
   Will go with you along.

We have short time to stay, as you,
   We have as short a spring;
As quick a growth to meet decay,
   As you, or any thing.
      We die,
   As your hours do, and dry
      Away,
   Like to the summer's rain;
Or as the pearls of morning's dew,
   Ne'er to be found again.

64

W. S. Gilbert
THE NIGHTMARE

When you're lying awake with a dismal headache, and repose is
    taboo'd by anxiety,
I conceive you may use any language you choose to indulge in,
    without impropriety;
For your brain is on fire – the bedclothes conspire of usual
    slumber to plunder you:
First your counterpane goes, and uncovers your toes, and your
    sheet slips demurely from under you;
Then the blanketing tickles – you feel like mixed pickles – so
    terribly sharp is the pricking,
And you're hot, and you're cross, and you tumble and toss till
    there's nothing 'twixt you and the ticking.
Then the bedclothes all creep to the ground in a heap, and you
    pick 'em all up in a tangle;
Next your pillow resigns and politely declines to remain at its
    usual angle!
Well, you get some repose in the form of a doze, with hot eye-
    balls and head ever aching,
But your slumbering teems with such horrible dreams that you'd
    very much better be waking;
For you dream you are crossing the Channel, and tossing about
    in a steamer from Harwich—
Which is something between a large bathing machine
and a very small second-class carriage—

And you're giving a treat (penny ice and cold meat) to a party
   of friends and relations—
They're a ravenous horde – and they all came on board at
   Sloane Square and South Kensington Stations.
And bound on that journey you find your attorney (who started
   that morning from Devon);
He's a bit undersized, and you don't feel surprised when he tells
   you he's only eleven.
Well, you're driving like mad with this singular lad (by-the-by
   the ship's now a four-wheeler),
And you're playing round games, and he calls you bad names
   when you tell him that 'ties pay the dealer';
But this you can't stand, so you throw up your hand, and you
   find you're as cold as an icicle,
In your shirt and your socks (the black silk with gold clocks),
   crossing Salisbury Plain on a bicycle:
And he and the crew are on bicycles too – which they've
   somehow or other invested in—
And he's telling the tars, all the particu*lars* of a company he's
   interested in—
It's a scheme of devices, to get at low prices, all goods from
   cough mixtures to cables
(Which tickled the sailors) by treating retailers, as though they
   were all vege*t*ables—
You get a good spadesman to plant a small tradesman, (first take
   off his boots with a boot-tree),
And his legs will take root, and his fingers will shoot, and they'll
   blossom and bud like a fruit-tree—

From the greengrocer tree you get grapes and green pea, cauli-
  flower, pineapple, and cranberries,
While the pastrycook plant, cherry brandy will grant, apple
  puffs, and three-corners, and banberries—
The shares are a penny, and ever so many are taken by
  Rothschild and Baring,
And just as a few are allotted to you, you awake with a shudder
  despairing—
You're a regular wreck, with a crick in your neck, and no
  wonder you snore, for your head's on the floor, and you've
  needles and pins from your soles to your shins, and your flesh
  is a-creep for your left leg's asleep, and you've cramp in your
  toes, and a fly on your nose, and some fluff in your lung, and
  a feverish tongue, and a thirst that's intense, and a general
  sense that you haven't been sleeping in clover;
But the darkness has passed, and it's daylight at last, and the
  night has been long – ditto ditto my song – and thank good-
  ness they're both of them over!

63

T. S. Eliot

THE LOVE SONG OF J. ALFRED PRUFROCK

S'io credesse che mia risposta fosse
A persona che mai tornasse al mondo,
Questa fiamma staria senza piu scosse.
Ma perciocche giammai di questo fondo
Non torno vivo alcun, s'i'odo il vero,
Senza tema d'infamia ti rispondo.

Let us go then, you and I,
When the evening is spread out against the sky
Like a patient etherised upon a table;
Let us go, through certain half-deserted streets,
The muttering retreats
Of restless nights in one-night cheap hotels
And sawdust restaurants with oyster-shells:
Streets that follow like a tedious argument
Of insidious intent
To lead you to an overwhelming question . . .
Oh, do not ask, 'What is it?'
Let us go and make our visit.

In the room the women come and go
Talking of Michelangelo.

76

The yellow fog that rubs its back upon the window-panes,
The yellow smoke that rubs its muzzle on the window-panes
Licked its tongue into the corners of the evening,
Lingered upon the pools that stand in drains,
Let fall upon its back the soot that falls from chimneys,
Slipped by the terrace, made a sudden leap,
And seeing that it was a soft October night,
Curled once about the house, and fell asleep.

And indeed there will be time
For the yellow smoke that slides along the street,
Rubbing its back upon the window-panes;
There will be time, there will be time
To prepare a face to meet the faces that you meet;
There will be time to murder and create,
And time for all the works and days of hands
That lift and drop a question on your plate;
Time for you and time for me,
And time yet for a hundred indecisions,
And for a hundred visions and revisions,
Before the taking of a toast and tea.

In the room the women come and go
Talking of Michelangelo.

And indeed there will be time
To wonder, 'Do I dare?' and, 'Do I dare?'
Time to turn back and descend the stair,
With a bald spot in the middle of my hair—
[They will say: 'How his hair is growing thin!']

My morning coat, my collar mounting firmly to the chin,
My necktie rich and modest, but asserted by a simple pin—
[They will say: 'But how his arms and legs are thin!']
Do I dare
Disturb the universe?
In a minute there is time
For decisions and revisions which a minute will reverse.

For I have known them all already, known them all—
Have known the evenings, mornings, afternoons,
I have measured out my life with coffee spoons;
I know the voices dying with a dying fall
Beneath the music from a farther room.
  So how should I presume?

And I have known the eyes already, known them all—
The eyes that fix you in a formulated phrase,
And when I am formulated, sprawling on a pin,
When I am pinned and wriggling on the wall,
Then how should I begin
To spit out all the butt-ends of my days and ways?
  And how should I presume?

And I have known the arms already, known them all—
Arms that are braceleted and white and bare
[But in the lamplight, downed with light brown hair!]
Is it perfume from a dress
That makes me so digress?
Arms that lie along a table, or wrap about a shawl.
  And should I then presume?
  And how should I begin?
        .   .   .   .   .

Shall I say, I have gone at dusk through narrow streets
And watched the smoke that rises from the pipes
Of lonely men in shirt-sleeves, leaning out of windows? . . .

I should have been a pair of ragged claws
Scuttling across the floors of silent seas.

. . . . .

And the afternoon, the evening, sleeps so peacefully!
Smoothed by long fingers,
Asleep . . . tired . . . or it malingers,
Stretched on the floor, here beside you and me.
Should I, after tea and cakes and ices,
Have the strength to force the moment to its crisis?
But though I have wept and fasted, wept and prayed,
Though I have seen my head [grown slightly bald] brought in
upon a platter,
I am no prophet—and here's no great matter;
I have seen the moment of my greatness flicker,
And I have seen the eternal Footman hold my coat, and snicker,
And in short, I was afraid.

And would it have been worth it, after all,
After the cups, the marmalade, the tea,
Among the porcelain, among some talk of you and me,
Would it have been worth while,
To have bitten off the matter with a smile,
To have squeezed the universe into a ball
To roll it toward some overwhelming question,
To say: 'I am Lazarus, come from the dead,
Come back to tell you all, I shall tell you all'—

If one, settling a pillow by her head,
  Should say: 'That is not what I meant at all.
  That is not it, at all.'

And would it have been worth it, after all,
Would it have been worth while,
After the sunsets and the dooryards and the sprinkled streets,
After the novels, after the teacups, after the skirts that trail along
    the floor—
And this, and so much more?—
It is impossible to say just what I mean!
But as if a magic lantern threw the nerves in patterns on a screen:
Would it have been worth while
If one, settling a pillow or throwing off a shawl,
And turning toward the window, should say:
  'That is not it at all,
  That is not what I meant, at all.'
            .   .   .   .

No! I am not Prince Hamlet, nor was meant to be;
Am an attendant lord, one that will do
To swell a progress, start a scene or two,
Advise the prince; no doubt, an easy tool,
Deferential, glad to be of use,
Politic, cautious, and meticulous;
Full of high sentence, but a bit obtuse;
At times, indeed, almost ridiculous—
Almost, at times, the Fool.

I grow old . . . I grow old . . .
I shall wear the bottoms of my trousers rolled.

Shall I part my hair behind? Do I dare to eat a peach?
I shall wear white flannel trousers, and walk upon the beach.
I have heard the mermaids singing, each to each.

I do not think that they will sing to me.

I have seen them riding seaward on the waves
Combing the white hair of the waves blown back
When the wind blows the water white and black.

We have lingered in the chambers of the sea
By sea-girls wreathed with seaweed red and brown
Till human voices wake us, and we drown.

John Donne

A VALEDICTION: FORBIDDING MOURNING

As virtuous men passe mildly away,
    And whisper to their soules, to goe,
Whilst some of their sad friends doe say,
    The breath goes now, and some say, no:

So let us melt, and make no noise,
    No teare-floods, nor sigh-tempests move,
'Twere prophanation of our joyes
    To tell the layetie our love.

Moving of th' earth brings harmes and feares,
    Men reckon what it did and meant,
But trepidation of the spheares,
    Though greater farre, is innocent.

Dull sublunary lovers' love
    (Whose soule is sense) cannot admit
Absence, because it doth remove
    Those things which elemented it.

But we by a love, so much refin'd,
    That our selves know not what it is,
Inter-assured of the mind,
    Care lesse, eyes, lips, and hands to misse.

Our two soules therefore, which are one,
    Though I must goe, endure not yet
A breach, but an expansion,
    Like gold to ayery thinnesse beate.

If they be two, they are two so
    As stiffe twin compasses are two,
Thy soule the fixt foot, makes no show
    To move, but doth, if th'other doe.

And though it in the centre sit,
    Yet when the other far doth rome,
It leanes, and hearkens after it,
    And growes erect, as that comes home.

Such wilt thou be to mee, who must
    Like th'other foot, obliquely runne;
Thy firmness makes my circle just,
    And makes me end, where I begunne.

Noël Coward
MAD DOGS AND ENGLISHMEN

In tropical climes there are certain times of day,
When all the citizens retire
To tear their clothes off and perspire.
It's one of those rules that the greatest fools obey,
Because the sun is much too sultry
And one must avoid its ultry-violet ray . . .
The natives grieve when the white men leave their huts,
Because they're obviously definitely nuts!

Mad dogs and Englishmen
Go out in the midday sun.
The Japanese don't care to,
The Chinese wouldn't dare to,
Hindoos and Argentines sleep firmly from twelve to one,
But Englishmen detest a
Siesta.
In the Philippines there are lovely screens
To protect you from the glare.
In the Malay States there are hats like plates
Which the Britishers wont wear.
At twelve noon
The natives swoon
And no further work is done,
But mad dogs and Englishmen
Go out in the midday sun.

It's such a surprise for the Eastern eyes to see,
That though the English are effete
They're quite impervious to heat.
When the white man rides every native hides in glee,
Because the simple creatures hope he
Will impale his solar topee on a tree . . .
It seems such a shame when the English claim the earth
That they give rise to such hilarity and mirth.

Mad dogs and Englishmen
Go out in the midday sun.
The toughest Burmese bandit
Can never understand it.
In Rangoon the heat of noon
Is just what the natives shun.
They put their Scotch or rye down
And lie down.
In a jungle town
Where the sun beats down
To the rage of man and beast,
The English garb
Of the English sahib
Merely gets a bit more creased.
In Bangkok
At twelve o'clock
They foam at the mouth and run,
But mad dogs and Englishmen
Go out in the midday sun.

60

Alan Ahlberg
PLEASE MRS BUTLER

Please Mrs Butler
This boy Derek Drew
Keeps copying my work, Miss.
What shall I do?

Go and sit in the hall, dear.
Go and sit in the sink.
Take your books on the roof, my lamb.
Do whatever you think.

Please Mrs Butler
This boy Derek Drew
Keeps taking my rubber, Miss.
What shall I do?

Keep it in your hand, dear.
Hide it up your vest.
Swallow it if you like, my love.
Do what you think best.

Please Mrs Butler
This boy Derek Drew
Keeps calling me rude names, Miss.
What shall I do?

Lock yourself in the cupboard, dear.
Run away to sea.
Do whatever you can, my flower.
But *don't ask me!*

William Wordsworth
THE SOLITARY REAPER

Behold her, single in the field,
Yon solitary Highland Lass!
Reaping and singing by herself;
Stop here, or gently pass!
Alone she cuts and binds the grain,
And sings a melancholy strain;
O listen! for the Vale profound
Is overflowing with the sound.

No Nightingale did ever chaunt
So sweetly to reposing bands
Of Travellers in some shady haunt,
Among Arabian Sands:
No sweeter voice was ever heard
In spring-time from the Cuckoo-bird,
Breaking the silence of the seas
Among the farthest Hebrides.

Will no one tell me what she sings? –
Perhaps the plaintive numbers flow
For old, unhappy, far-off things,
And battles long ago:
Or is it some more humble lay,

Familiar matter of today
Some natural sorrow, loss or pain,
That has been, and may be again!

Whate'er the theme, the Maiden sang
As if her song could have no ending;
I saw her singing at her work,
And o'er the sickle bending;
I listened till I had my fill:
And, as I mounted up the hill,
The music in my heart I bore,
Long after it was heard no more.

Dylan Thomas
DO NOT GO GENTLE INTO THAT GOOD NIGHT

Do not go gentle into that good night,
Old age should burn and rave at close of day;
Rage, rage against the dying of the light.

Though wise men at their end know dark is right,
Because their words had forked no lightning they
Do not go gentle into that good night.

Good men, the last wave by, crying how bright
Their frail deeds might have danced in a green bay,
Rage, rage against the dying of the light.

Wild men who caught and sang the sun in flight,
And learn, too late, they grieved it on its way,
Do not go gentle into that good night.

Grave men, near death, who see with blinding sight
Blind eyes could blaze like meteors and be gay,
Rage, rage against the dying of the light.

And you, my father, there on the sad height,
Curse, bless, me now with your fierce tears, I pray.
Do not go gentle into that good night.
Rage, rage against the dying of the light.

57

Sir Henry Newbolt
VITAÏ LAMPADA

There's a breathless hush in the Close to-night –
    Ten to make and the match to win –
A bumping pitch and a blinding light,
    An hour to play and the last man in.
And it's not for the sake of a ribboned coat,
    Or the selfish hope of a season's fame,
But his Captain's hand on his shoulder smote –
    'Play up! play up! and play the game!'

The sand of the desert is sodden red, –
    Red with the wreck of a square that broke; –
The Gatling's jammed and the Colonel dead,
    And the regiment blind with dust and smoke.
The river of death has brimmed his banks,
    And England's far, and Honour a name,
But the voice of a schoolboy rallies the ranks:
    'Play up! play up! and play the game!'

This is the word that year by year,
    While in her place the School is set,
Every one of her sons must hear,
    And none that hears it dare forget.
This they all with a joyful mind

Bear through life like a torch in flame,
And falling fling to the host behind –
'Play up! play up! and play the game!'

56

Henry Wadsworth Longfellow
A PSALM OF LIFE
WHAT THE HEART OF THE YOUNG MAN SAID TO THE PSALMIST

Tell me not, in mournful numbers,
  'Life is but an empty dream!'
For the soul is dead that slumbers,
  And things are not what they seem.

Life is real! Life is earnest!
  And the grave is not its goal;
'Dust thou art, to dust returnest'
  Was not spoken of the soul.

Not enjoyment, and not sorrow,
  Is our destined end or way;
But to act, that each to-morrow
  Find us farther than to-day.

Art is long, and Time is fleeting,
  And our hearts, though stout and brave,
Still, like muffled drums, are beating
  Funeral marches to the grave.

In the world's broad field of battle,
  In the bivouac of Life,

Be not like dumb, driven cattle!
  Be a hero in the strife!

Trust no Future, howe'er pleasant!
  Let the dead Past bury its dead!
Act – act in the living Present!
  Heart within, and God o'erhead!

Lives of great men all remind us
  We can make our lives sublime,
And, departing, leave behind us
  Footprints on the sands of time; –

Footprints, that perhaps another,
  Sailing o'er life's solemn main,
A forlorn and shipwrecked brother,
  Seeing, shall take heart again.

Let us, then, be up and doing,
  With a heart for any fate;
Still achieving, still pursuing,
  Learn to labour and to wait.

55

John Keats
LA BELLE DAME SANS MERCI

'O what can ail thee, knight-at-arms,
   Alone and palely loitering?
The sedge has wither'd from the lake,
      And no birds sing.

'O what can ail thee, knight-at-arms!
   So haggard and so woe-begone?
The squirrel's granary is full,
   And the harvest's done.

'I see a lily on thy brow
   With anguish moist and fever-dew,
And on thy cheeks a fading rose
   Fast withereth too.'

'I met a lady in the meads,
   Full beautiful – a faery's child,
Her hair was long, her foot was light,
   And her eyes were wild.

'I made a garland for her head,
    And bracelets too, and fragrant zone;
She look'd at me as she did love,
    And made sweet moan.

'I set her on my pacing steed
    And nothing else saw all day long,
For sidelong would she bend, and sing
    A faery's song.

'She found me roots of relish sweet,
    And honey wild and manna-dew,
And sure in language strange she said
        "I love thee true."

'She took me to her elfin grot,
    And there she wept, and sigh'd full sore,
And there I shut her wild wild eyes
    With kisses four.

'And there she lulled me asleep
    And there I dream'd – Ah! Woe betide!
The latest dream I ever dream'd
    On the cold hill side.

'I saw pale kings and princes too,
    Pale warriors, death-pale were they all;
They cried – "La Belle Dame sans Merci
        Hath thee in thrall!"

'I saw their starv'd lips in the gloam
　　With horrid warning gapèd wide,
And I awoke and found me here
　　On the cold hill's side.

'And this is why I sojourn here
　　Alone and palely loitering,
Though the sedge is wither'd from the lake
　　And no birds sing.'

Leigh Hunt
ABOU BEN ADHEM

Abou Ben Adhem (may his tribe increase!)
Awoke one night from a deep dream of peace,
And saw, within the moonlight in his room,
Making it rich, and like a lily in bloom,
An angel writing in a book of gold: –
Exceeding peace had made Ben Adhem bold,
And to the presence in the room he said,
    'What writest thou?' – The vision raised its head,
And with a look made of all sweet accord,
Answered, 'The names of those who love the Lord.'
'And is mine one?' said Abou. 'Nay, not so,'
Replied the angel. Abou spoke more low,
But cheerly still; and said, 'I pray thee, then,
Write me as one that loves his fellow-men.'
    The angel wrote, and vanished. The next night
It came again with a great wakening light,
And showed the names whom love of God had blest,
And lo! Ben Adhem's name led all the rest.

53

Thomas Hardy
WEATHERS

This is the weather the cuckoo likes,
   And so do I;
When showers betumble the chestnut spikes,
   And nestlings fly:
And the little brown nightingale bills his best,
And they sit outside at 'The Travellers' Rest',
And maids come forth sprig-muslin drest,
And citizens dream of the south and west,
   And so do I.

This is the weather the shepherd shuns,
   And so do I;
When beeches drip in brown and duns,
   And thresh, and ply;
And hill-hid tides throb, throe on throe,
And meadow rivulets overflow,
And drops on gate-bars hang in a row,
And rooks in families homeward go,
   And so do I.

W. S. Gilbert

THE MODERN MAJOR-GENERAL

I am the very pattern of a modern Major-Gineral,
I've information vegetable, animal, and mineral;
I know the kings of England, and I quote the fights historical,
From Marathon to Waterloo, in order categorical;
I'm very well acquainted, too, with matters mathematical,
I understand equations, both the simple and quadratical;
About binomial theorem I'm teeming with a lot o' news,
With interesting facts about the square of the hypotenuse.
I'm very good at integral and differential calculus,
I know the scientific names of beings animalculous.
In short, in matters vegetable, animal, and mineral,
I am the very model of a modern Major-Gineral.

I know our mythic history – KING ARTHUR's and SIR
    CARADOC's,
I answer hard acrostics, I've a pretty taste for paradox;
I quote in elegiacs all the crimes of HELIOGABALUS,
In conics I can floor peculiarities parabolous.
I tell undoubted RAPHAELS from GERARD DOWS and ZOFFANIES,
I know the croaking chorus from the 'Frogs' of ARISTOPHANES;
Then I can hum a fugue, of which I've heard the music's din afore,
And whistle all the airs from that confounded nonsense
    'Pinafore.'

Then I can write a washing-bill in Babylonic cuneiform,
And tell you every detail of CARACTACUS's uniform.
In short, in matters vegetable, animal, and mineral,
I am the very model of a modern Major-Gineral.

In fact, when I know what is meant by 'mamelon' and 'ravelin,'
When I can tell at sight a Chassepôt rifle from a javelin,
When such affairs as *sorties* and surprises I'm more wary at,
And when I know precisely what is meant by Commissariat,
When I have learnt what progress has been made in modern
    gunnery,
When I know more of tactics than a novice in a nunnery,
In short, when Ive a smattering of elementary strategy,
You'll say a better Major-Gine*ral* has never *sat* a gee—
For my military knowledge, though I'm plucky and adventury,
Has only been brought down to the beginning of the century.
But still in learning vegetable, animal, and mineral,
I am the very model of a modern Major-Gineral!

T. S. Eliot

SKIMBLESHANKS: THE RAILWAY CAT

There's a whisper down the line at 11.39
When the Night Mail's ready to depart,
Saying 'Skimble where is Skimble has he gone to hunt the
    thimble?
We must find him or the train can't start.'
All the guards and all the porters and the stationmaster's
    daughters
They are searching high and low,
Saying 'Skimble where is Skimble for unless he's very nimble
Then the Night Mail just can't go.'
At 11.42 then the signal's nearly due
And the passengers are frantic to a man—
Then Skimble will appear and he'll saunter to the rear:
He's been busy in the luggage van!
   He gives one flash of his glass-green eyes
      And the signal goes 'All Clear!'
   And we're off at last for the northern part
      Of the Northern Hemisphere!

You may say that by and large it is Skimble who's in charge
Of the Sleeping Car Express.
From the driver and the guards to the bagmen playing cards
He will supervise them all, more or less.

Down the corridor he paces and examines all the faces
Of the travellers in the First and in the Third;
He establishes control by a regular patrol
And he'd know at once if anything occurred.
He will watch you without winking and he sees what you are
    thinking
And it's certain that he doesn't approve
Of hilarity and riot, so the folk are very quiet
When Skimble is about and on the move.
    You can play no pranks with Skimbleshanks!
      He's a Cat that cannot be ignored;
   So nothing goes wrong on the Northern Mail
      When Skimbleshanks is aboard.

Oh it's very pleasant when you have found your little den
With your name written up on the door.
And the berth is very neat with a newly folded sheet
And there's not a speck of dust on the floor.
There is every sort of light – you can make it dark or bright;
There's a handle that you turn to make a breeze.
There's a funny little basin you're supposed to wash your face in
And a crank to shut the window if you sneeze.
Then the guard looks in politely and will ask you very brightly
'Do you like your morning tea weak or strong?'
But Skimbles just behind him and was ready to remind him,
For Skimble won't let anything go wrong.
    And when you creep into your cosy berth
      And pull up the counterpane,
   You ought to reflect that it's very nice
   To know that you won't be bothered by mice—

You can leave all that to the Railway Cat,
  The Cat of the Railway Train!

In the watches of the night he is always fresh and bright;
Every now and then he has a cup of tea
With perhaps a drop of Scotch while he's keeping on the watch,
Only stopping here and there to catch a flea.
You were fast asleep at Crewe and so you never knew
That he was walking up and down the station;
You were sleeping all the while he was busy at Carlisle,
Where he greets the stationmaster with elation.
But you saw him at Dumfries, where he speaks to the police
If there's anything they ought to know about:
When you get to Gallowgate there you do not have to wait—
For Skimbleshanks will help you to get out!
  He gives you a wave of his long brown tail
    Which says: 'I'll see you again!
  You'll meet without fail on the Midnight Mail
    The cat of the Railway Train.'

Christopher Marlowe
THE PASSIONATE SHEPHERD TO HIS LOVE

Come live with me and be my Love,
And we will all the pleasures prove
That hills and valleys, dales and fields,
And all the craggy mountains yields.

There we will sit upon the rocks
And see the shepherds feed their flocks,
By shallow rivers, to whose falls
Melodious birds sing madrigals.

And I will make thee beds of roses
And a thousand fragrant posies,
A cap of flowers, and a kirtle
Embroider'd all with leaves of myrtle.

A gown made of the finest wool,
Which from our pretty lambs we pull,
Fair lined slippers for the cold,
With buckles of the purest gold.

A belt of straw and ivy buds
With coral clasps and amber studs:
And if these pleasures may thee move,
Come live with me and be my Love.

Thy silver dishes for thy meat
As precious as the gods do eat,
Shall on an ivory table be
Prepared each day for thee and me.

The shepherd swains shall dance and sing
For thy delight each May-morning:
If these delights thy mind may move,
Then live with me and be my Love.

49

Nigel Forde
SEA FRET

I must down to the seas again,
To the lonely sea and the sky,
Where half a million shoulderblades
Are oiled and ready to fry;
And bodies that winter has gratefully veiled
Come out and appal the eye;

And father is bluff and hearty and scoffs:
'Just a crab! Pick it up! Be a man!'
And he picks it up with a chuckle of scorn
And loses the use of one hand;
And grandmother ponders the memories brought
By a gusset full of sand;

And the local youths have constructed a goal
Out of jackets and cans of beer;
'To me! Barry! To me! To me!
Barry! To me! Over here!'
And the girls, unimpressed go on building a nest
Of crash-helmets and Ambre-Solaire;

While the wholemeal parents have taken Cassandra
For an ecological spin

To the farming museum, the butterfly park
And the oak that cloaked a King,
When all she wants is a bucket and spade
And a friend with a cockney grin;

And Kevin, by accident, brushes the hand
Of his next-door neighbour's daughter
Who watches the tide receding as fast
As the things that her mother has taught her,
And the darkling beach spins a long double line
Of footprints filling with water;

And the boarding-house smell (of wet plimsolls and gas
And polish) pervades the gloom
Where father watches the Test highlights
In the bare little TV room;
And mother is hopeful in underwear
Like she wore on her honeymoon;

And when it's all over, the luggage is lugged,
And everyone's tired and snappy,
For they got up to pack at a quarter past five
And the baby's just filled his fourth nappy;
Was it worth all the bother? For only the dog
Has been *truly* and *blissfully* happy.

48

John Donne
THE GOOD-MORROW

I wonder by my troth, what thou, and I
   Did, till we lov'd? were we not wean'd till then?
But suck'd on countrey pleasures, childishly?
   Or snorted we in the seven sleepers' den?
'Twas so; but this, all pleasures fancies bee;
If ever any beauty I did see,
Which I desir'd, and got, 'twas but a dreame of thee.

And now good morrow to our waking soules,
   Which watch not one another out of feare;
For love, all love of other sights controules,
   And makes one little roome an every where.
Let sea-discoverers to new worlds have gone,
Let maps to others, worlds on worlds have showne,
Let us possesse one world, each hath one, and is one.

My face in thine eye, thine in mine appeares,
   And true plaine hearts doe in the faces rest,
Where can we finde two better hemispheares
   Without sharpe North, without declining West?
What ever dyes, was not mixt equally;
If our two loves be one, or thou and I
Love so alike, that none doe slacken, none can die.

47

Lewis Carroll
THE WALRUS AND THE CARPENTER

The sun was shining on the sea,
 Shining with all his might:
He did his very best to make
 The billows smooth and bright—
And this was odd, because it was
 The middle of the night.

The moon was shining sulkily,
 Because she thought the sun
Had got no business to be there
 After the day was done—
'It's very rude of him,' she said,
 'To come and spoil the fun!'

The sea was wet as wet could be,
 The sands were dry as dry.
You could not see a cloud, because
 No cloud was in the sky:
No birds were flying overhead—
 There were no birds to fly.

The Walrus and the Carpenter
 Were walking close at hand:

They wept like anything to see
   Such quantities of sand:
'If this were only cleared away,'
   They said, 'it would be grand!'

'If seven maids with seven mops
   Swept it for half a year,
Do you suppose,' the Walrus said,
   'That they could get it clear?'
'I doubt it,' said the Carpenter,
   And shed a bitter tear.

'O Oysters, come and walk with us!'
   The Walrus did beseech.
'A pleasant walk, a pleasant talk,
   Along the briny beach:
We cannot do with more than four,
   To give a hand to each.'

The eldest Oyster looked at him,
   But never a word he said:
The eldest Oyster winked his eye,
   And shook his heavy head—
Meaning to say he did not choose
   To leave the oyster-bed.

But four young Oysters hurried up,
   All eager for the treat:
Their coats were brushed, their faces washed,
   Their shoes were clean and neat—

And this was odd, because you know,
   They hadn't any feet.

Four other Oysters followed them,
   And yet another four;
And thick and fast they came at last,
   And more, and more, and more—
All hopping through the frothy waves,
   And scrambling to the shore.

The Walrus and the Carpenter
   Walked on a mile or so,
And then they rested on a rock
   Conveniently low:
And all the little Oysters stood
   And waited in a row.

'The time has come,' the Walrus said,
   'To talk of many things:
Of shoes – and ships – and sealing wax—
   Of cabbages – and kings—
And why the sea is boiling hot—
   And whether pigs have wings.'

'But wait a bit,' the Oysters cried,
   'Before we have our chat;
For some of us are out of breath,
   And all of us are fat!'
'No hurry!' said the Carpenter.
   They thanked him much for that.

'A loaf of bread,' the Walrus said,
  'Is what we chiefly need:
Pepper and vinegar besides
  Are very good indeed—
Now, if you're ready, Oysters dear
  We can begin to feed.'

'But not on us!' the Oysters cried,
  Turning a little blue.
'After such kindness, that would be
  A dismal thing to do!'
'The night is fine,' the Walrus said,
  'Do you admire the view?

'It was so kind of you to come!
  And you are very nice!'
The Carpenter said nothing but
  'Cut us another slice.
I wish you were not quite so deaf—
  I've had to ask you twice!'

'It seems a shame,' the Walrus said,
  'To play them such a trick.
After we've brought them out so far,
  And made them trot so quick!'
The Carpenter said nothing but
  'The butter's spread too thick!'

'I weep for you,' the Walrus said:
  'I deeply sympathize.'

With sobs and tears he sorted out
    Those of the largest size,
Holding his pocket-handkerchief
    Before his streaming eyes.

'O Oysters,' said the Carpenter,
    'You've had a pleasant run!
Shall we be trotting home again!'
    But answer came there none—
And this was scarcely odd, because
    They'd eaten every one.

46

Alfred Noyes
THE HIGHWAYMAN

The wind was a torrent of darkness among the gusty trees,
The moon was a ghostly galleon tossed upon cloudy seas,
The road was a ribbon of moonlight looping the purple moor,
And the highwayman came riding –
    Riding – riding –
The highwayman came riding, up to the old inn door.

He'd a French cocked hat on his forehead, and a bunch of lace
   at his chin;
He'd a coat of the claret velvet, and breeches of fine doe-skin.
They fitted with never a wrinkle; his boots were up to his thigh!
And he rode with a jewelled twinkle –
    His rapier hilt a-twinkle –
His pistol butts a-twinkle, under the jewelled sky.

Over the cobbles he clattered and clashed in the dark inn-yard,
He tapped with his whip on the shutters, but all was locked and
   barred,
He whistled a tune to the window, and who should be waiting
   there

But the landlord's black-eyed daughter –
    Bess, the landlord's daughter –
Plaiting a dark red love-knot into her long black hair.

Dark in the old inn-yard a stable-wicket creaked
Where Tim the ostler listened – his face was white and peaked –
His eyes were hollows of madness, his hair like mouldy hay,
But he loved the landlord's daughter –
    The landlord's black-eyed daughter;
Dumb as a dog he listened, and he heard the robber say:

'One kiss, my bonny sweetheart; I'm after a prize tonight,
But I shall be back with the yellow gold before the morning light.
Yet if they press me sharply, and harry me through the day,
Then look for me by moonlight,
    Watch for me by moonlight,
I'll come to thee by moonlight, though hell should bar the way.'

He stood upright in the stirrups; he scarce could reach her hand,
But she loosened her hair in the casement! His face burnt like a
    brand
As the sweet black waves of perfume came tumbling o'er his
    breast,
Then he kissed its waves in the moonlight
    (O sweet black waves in the moonlight!),
And he tugged at his reins in the moonlight, and galloped away
    to the west.

He did not come in the dawning; he did not come at noon.
And out of the tawny sunset, before the rise of the moon,

116

When the road was a gypsy's ribbon over the purple moor,
The redcoat troops came marching –
Marching – marching –
King George's men came marching, up to the old inn-door.

They said no word to the landlord; they drank his ale instead,
But they gagged his daughter and bound her to the foot of her
    narrow bed.
Two of them knelt at her casement, with muskets by their side;
There was Death at every window,
And Hell at one dark window,
For Bess could see, through her casement, the road that he
    would ride.

They had bound her up at attention, with many a sniggering jest!
They had tied a rifle beside her, with the barrel beneath her
    breast!
'Now keep good watch!' and they kissed her. She heard the dead
    man say,
'Look for me by moonlight,
Watch for me by moonlight,
I'll come to thee by moonlight, though Hell should bar the way.'

She twisted her hands behind her, but all the knots held good!
She writhed her hands till her fingers were wet with sweat or blood!
They stretched and strained in the darkness, and the hours
    crawled by like years,
Till, on the stroke of midnight,
Cold on the stroke of midnight,
The tip of one finger touched it! The trigger at least was hers!

The tip of one finger touched it, she strove no more for the rest;
Up, she stood up at attention, with the barrel beneath her breast.
She would not risk their hearing, she would not strive again,
For the road lay bare in the moonlight,
Blank and bare in the moonlight,
And the blood in her veins, in the moonlight, throbbed to her
   love's refrain.

Tlot tlot, tlot tlot! Had they heard it? The horse-hooves, ringing
   clear;
Tlot tlot, tlot tlot, in the distance! Were they deaf that they did
   not hear?
Down the ribbon of moonlight, over the brow of the hill,
The highwayman came riding –
Riding – riding –
The redcoats looked to their priming! She stood up straight and
   still.

Tlot tlot, in the frosty silence! Tlot tlot, in the echoing night!
Nearer he came and nearer! Her face was like a light!
Her eyes grew wide for a moment, she drew one last deep breath,
Then her finger moved in the moonlight –
Her musket shattered the moonlight –
Shattered her breast in the moonlight and warned him – with
   her death.

He turned, he spurred to the West; he did not know who stood
Bowed, with her head o'er the casement, drenched in her own
   red blood!
Not till the dawn did he hear it, and his face grew grey to hear

How Bess, the landlord's daughter,
The landlord's black-eyed daughter,
Had watched for her love in the moonlight, and died in the
    darkness there.

Back, he spurred like a madman, shrieking a curse to the sky,
With the white road smoking behind him and his rapier
    brandished high!
Blood-red were his spurs in the golden noon, wine-red was his
    velvet coat
When they shot him down in the highway,
Down like a dog in the highway,
And he lay in his blood in the highway, with the bunch of lace
    at his throat.

And still on a winter's night, they say, when the wind is in the
    trees,
When the moon is a ghostly galleon tossed upon cloudy seas,
When the road is a gypsy's ribbon looping the purple moor,
The highwayman comes riding –
Riding – riding –
The highwayman comes riding, up to the old inn-door.

Over the cobbles he clatters and clangs in the dark inn-yard,
He taps with his whip on the shutters, but all is locked and barred,
He whistles a tune to the window, and who should be waiting
    there
But the landlord's black-eyed daughter –
Bess, the landlord's daughter –
Plaiting a dark red love-knot into her long black hair.

45

John Gillespie Magee
HIGH FLIGHT

Oh, I have slipped the surly bonds of earth
And danced the skies on laughter-silvered wings;
Sunward I've climbed and joined the tumbling mirth
Of sun-split clouds – and done a hundred things
You have not dreamed of; wheeled and soared and swung
High in the sun-lit silence. Hovering there
I've chased the shouting wind along, and flung
My eager craft through footless halls of air;
Up, up the long, delirious, burning blue
I've topped the wind-swept heights with easy grace,
Where never lark nor even eagle flew;
And while, with silent lifting mind I've trod
The high untrespassed sanctity of space,
Put out my hand, and touched the face of God.

44

Rudyard Kipling

THE GLORY OF THE GARDEN

Our England is a garden that is full of stately views,
Of borders, beds and shrubberies and lawns and avenues,
With statues on the terraces and peacocks strutting by;
But the Glory of the Garden lies in more than meets the eye.

For where the old thick laurels grow, along the thin red wall,
You find the tool- and potting-sheds which are the heart of all;
The cold-frames and the hot-houses, the dungpits and the tanks,
The rollers, carts and drain-pipes, with the barrows and the
    planks.

And there you'll see the gardeners, the men and 'prentice boys
Told off to do as they are bid and do it without noise;
For, except when seeds are planted and we shout to scare the
    birds,
The Glory of the Garden it abideth not in words.

And some can pot begonias and some can bud a rose,
And some are hardly fit to trust with anything that grows;
But they can roll and trim the lawns and sift the sand and loam,
For the Glory of the Garden occupieth all who come.

Our England is a garden, and such gardens are not made
By singing:– 'Oh, how beautiful!' and sitting in the shade,
While better men than we go out and start their working lives
At grubbing weeds from gravel-paths with broken dinner-knives.

There's not a pair of legs so thin, there's not a head so thick,
There's not a hand so weak and white, nor yet a heart so sick,
But it can find some needful job that's crying to be done,
For the Glory of the Garden glorifieth every one.

Then seek your job with thankfulness and work till further
    orders,
If it's only netting strawberries or killing slugs on borders;
And when your back stops aching and your hands begin to
    harden,
You will find yourself a partner in the Glory of the Garden.

Oh, Adam was a gardener, and God who made him sees
That half a proper gardener's work is done upon his knees,
So when your work is finished, you can wash your hands and
    pray
For the Glory of the Garden, that it may not pass away!
And the Glory of the Garden it shall never pass away!

43

Rudyard Kipling
THE WAY THROUGH THE WOODS

('Marklake Witches' – *Rewards and Fairies*)

They shut the road through the woods
Seventy years ago.
Weather and rain have undone it again,
And now you would never know
There was once a road through the woods
Before they planted the trees.
It is underneath the coppice and heath
And the thin anemones.
Only the keeper sees
That, where the ring-dove broods,
And the badgers roll at ease,
There was once a road through the woods.

Yet, if you enter the woods
Of a summer evening late,
When the night-air cools on the trout-ringed pools
Where the otter whistles his mate,
(They fear not men in the woods,
Because they see so few.)
You will hear the beat of a horse's feet,
And the swish of a skirt in the dew,

Steadily cantering through
The misty solitudes,
As though they perfectly knew
The old lost road through the woods . . .
But there is no road through the woods.

42

Francis Thompson
THE HOUND OF HEAVEN

I fled Him, down the nights and down the days;
 I fled Him down the arches of the years;
I fled Him. Down the labyrinthine ways
 Of my own mind; and in the mist of tears
I hid from Him, and under running laughter.
        Up vistaed hopes I sped;
        And shot, precipitated.
Adown Titanic glooms of chasmèd fears,
 From those strong Feet that followed, followed after.
    But with unhurrying chase,
    And unperturbed pace,
Deliberate speed, majestic instancy
    They beat – and a Voice beat
    More instant than the Feet –
'All things betray thee, who betrayest Me.'

    I pleaded, outlaw-wise,
By many a hearted casement, curtained red,
    Trellised with intertwining charities;
(For, though I knew His love Who followèd,
    Yet was I sore adread
Lest, having Him, I must have naught beside);
But, if one little casement parted wide,

The gust of His approach would clash it to.
Fear wist not to evade, as Love wist to pursue.
Across the margent of the world I fled,
   And troubled the gold gateways of the stars,
   Smiting for shelter on their clangèd bars;
     Fretted to dulcet jars
And silvern chatter the pale ports o' the moon.
I said to dawn, Be sudden; to eve, Be soon;
   With thy young skiey blossoms heap me over
      From this tremendous Lover!
Float thy vague veil about me, lest He see!
  I tempted all His servitors, but to find
My own betrayal in their constancy,
In faith to Him their fickleness to me,
   Their traitorous trueness, and their loyal deceit.
To all swift things for swiftness did I sue;
Clung to the whistling mane of every wind.
   But whether they swept, smoothly fleet,
   The long savannahs of the blue;
     Or whether, Thunder-driven,
   They clanged his chariot 'thwart a heaven
Plashy with flying lightnings round the spurn o' their feet:
   Fear wist not to evade as Love wist to pursue.

     Still with unhurrying chase,

     And unperturbed pace,
Deliberate speed, majestic instancy,
    Came on the following Feet,
    And a Voice above their beat –
'Naught shelters thee who wilt not shelter Me.'

Now of that long pursuit
        Comes on at hand the bruit:
That Voice is round me like a bursting sea:
        'And is thy earth so marred,
        Shattered in shard on shard?
Lo, all things fly thee, for thou fliest Me!
        Strange, piteous, futile thing,
Wherefore should any set thee love apart?
Seeing none but I makes much of naught' (He said)
'And human love needs human meriting:
        How hast thou merited –
Of all man's clotted clay the dingiest clot?
        Alack, thou knowest not
How little worthy of any love thou art!
Whom wilt thou find to love ignoble thee
        Save Me, save only Me?
All which I took from thee I did but take,
        Not for thy harms,
But just that thou might'st seek it in My arms.
        All which thy child's mistake
Fancies as lost, I have stored for thee at home:
        Rise, clasp My hand, and come!'

        Halts by me that footfall:
        Is my gloom, after all,
Shade of His hand, outstretched caressingly?
        'Ah, fondest, blindest, weakest,
        I am He Whom thou seekest!
Thou dravest love from thee, who dravest Me.'

41

Percy Bysshe Shelley
TO A SKYLARK

Hail to thee, blithe Spirit!
  Bird thou never wert,
That from Heaven, or near it,
  Pourest thy full heart
In profuse strains of unpremeditated art.

Higher still and higher
  From the earth thou springest
Like a cloud of fire;
  The blue deep thou wingest,
And singing still dost soar, and soaring ever singest.

In the golden lightning
  Of the sunken sun,
O'er which clouds are bright'ning,
  Thou dost float and run;
Like an unbodied joy whose race is just begun.

The pale purple even
  Melts around thy flight;
Like a star of Heaven,
  In the broad daylight
Thou art unseen, but yet I hear thy shrill delight,

Keen as are the arrows
  Of that silver sphere,
Whose intense lamp narrows
  In the white dawn clear
Until we hardly see – we feel that it is there.

All the earth and air
  With thy voice is loud,
As, when night is bare,
  From one lonely cloud
The moon rains out her beams, and Heaven is overflowed.

What thou art we know not;
  What is most like thee?
From rainbow clouds there flow not
  Drops so bright to see
As from thy presence showers a rain of melody.

Like a Poet hidden
  In the light of thought,
Singing hymns unbidden,
  Till the world is wrought
To sympathy with hopes and fears it heeded not:

Like a high-born maiden
  In a palace-tower,
Soothing her love-laden
  Soul in secret hour
With music sweet as love, which overflows her bower:

Like a glow-worm golden
    In a dell of dew,
Scattering unbeholden
    Its äreal hue
Among the flowers and grass, which screen it from the view!

Like a rose embowered
    In its own green leaves,
By warm winds deflowered,
    Till the scent it gives
Makes faint with too much sweet those heavy-wingèd thieves:

Sound of vernal showers
    On the twinkling grass,
Rain-awakened flowers,
    All that ever was
Joyous, and clear, and fresh, thy music doth surpass:

Teach us, Sprite or Bird,
    What sweet thoughts are thine:
I have never heard
    Praise of love or wine
That panted forth a flood of rapture so divine.

Chorus Hymeneal,
    Or triumphal chant,
Matched with thine would be all
    But an empty vaunt,
A thing wherein we feel there is some hidden want.

What objects are the fountains
    Of thy happy strain?
What fields, or waves, or mountains?
    What shapes of sky or plain?
What love of thine own kind? what ignorance of pain?

With thy clear keen joyance
    Languor cannot be:
Shadow of annoyance
    Never came near thee:
Thou lovest – but ne'er knew love's sad satiety.

Waking or asleep,
    Thou of death must deem
Things more true and deep
    Than we mortals dream,
Or how could thy notes flow in such a crystal stream?

We look before and after,
    And pine for what is not:
Our sincerest laughter
    With some pain is fraught;
Our sweetest songs are those that tell of saddest thought.

Yet if we could scorn
    Hate, and pride, and fear;
If we were things born
    Not to shed a tear,
I know not how thy joy we ever should come near.
Better than all measures

Of delightful sound,
Better than all treasures
    That in books are found,
Thy skill to poet were, thou scorner of the ground!

Teach me half the gladness
    That thy brain must know,
Such harmonious madness
    From my lips would flow
The world should listen then – as I am listening now.

40

Robert Burns
TO A MOUSE

Wee sleeket, cow'rin', tim'rous beastie,
O, what a panic's in thy breastie!
Thou need na start awa' sae hasty,
              Wi' bickerin' brattle!
I wad be laith to rin an' chase thee
               Wi' murderin' pattle!

I'm truly sorry man's dominion,
Has broken nature's social union,
An' justifies that ill opinion,
              Which makes thee startle
At me, thy poor, earth-born companion,
             An' fellow-mortal!

I doubt na, whyles, but thou may thieve;
What then? poor beastie, thou maun live!
A daimen icker in a thrave
             'S a sma' request;
I'll get a blessin' wi' the lave,
             An' never miss't!

Thy wee bit housie, too, in ruin!
Its silly wa's the win's are strewin'!
An' naething, now, to big a new ane,

O' foggage green!
An' bleak December's winds ensuin',
Baith snell an' keen!

Thou saw the fields laid bare an' waste,
An' weary winter comin' fast,
An' cozie here, beneath the blast,
Thou thought to dwell –
Till crash! the cruel coulter past
Out thro' thy cell.

That wee bit heap o' leaves an' stibble,
Has cost thee mony a weary nibble!
Now thou's turn'd out, for a' thy trouble,
But house or hald,
To thole the winter's sleety dribble,
An' crancreuch cauld!

But Mousie, thou art no thy lane,
In proving foresight may be vain;
The best-laid schemes o' mice an' men
Gang aft agley,
An' lea'e us nought but grief an' pain,
For promis'd joy!

Still thou art blest, compar'd wi' me!
The present only toucheth thee:
But och! I backward cast my e'e,
On prospects drear!
An' forward, tho' I canna see,
I guess an' fear!

39

Robert Browning
(FROM) MY LAST DUCHESS

That's my last Duchess painted on the wall,
Looking as if she were alive. I call
That piece a wonder, now: Frà Pandolf's hands
Worked busily a day, and there she stands.
Will't please you sit and look at her? I said
'Frà Pandolf' by design, for never read
Strangers like you that pictured countenance,
The depth and passion of its earnest glance,
But to myself they turned (since none puts by
The curtain I have drawn for you, but I)
And seemed as they would ask me, if they durst,
How such a glance came there; so, not the first
Are you to turn and ask thus. Sir, 'twas not
Her husband's presence only, called that spot
Of joy into the Duchess' cheek: perhaps
Frà Pandolf chanced to say 'Her mantle laps
Over my lady's wrist too much,' or 'Paint
Must never hope to reproduce the faint
Half-flush that dies along her throat:' such stuff
Was courtesy, she thought, and cause enough
For calling up that spot of joy. She had
A heart – how shall I say? – too soon made glad,

Too easily impressed; she liked whate'er
She looked on, and her looks went everywhere.
Sir, 'twas all one! My favour at her breast,
The dropping of the daylight in the West,
The bough of cherries some officious fool
Broke in the orchard for her, the white mule
She rode with round the terrace – all and each
Would draw from her alike the approving speech,
Or blush, at least. She thanked men, – good! but thanked
Somehow – I know not how – as if she ranked
My gift of a nine-hundred-years-old name
With anybody's gift.
Oh sir, she smiled, no doubt,
Whene'er I passed her; but who passed without
Much the same smile? This grew; I gave commands;
Then all smiles stopped together. There she stands
As if alive. Will't please you rise? We'll meet
The company below then. I repeat,
The Count your master's known munificence
Is ample warrant that no just pretence
Of mine for dowry will be disallowed;
Though his fair daughter's self, as I avowed
At starting, is my object. Nay, we'll go
Together down, sir. Notice Neptune, though,
Taming a sea-horse, thought a rarity,
Which Claus of Innsbruck cast in bronze for me!

38

Walter De La Mare
THE LISTENERS

'Is there anybody there?' said the Traveller,
  Knocking on the moonlit door;
And his horse in the silence champed the grasses
  Of the forest's ferny floor:
And a bird flew up out of the turret,
  Above the Traveller's head:
And he smote upon the door again a second time;
  'Is there anybody there?' he said.
But no one descended to the Traveller;
  No head from the leaf-fringed sill
Leaned over and looked into his grey eyes,
  Where he stood perplexed and still.
But only a host of phantom listeners
  That dwelt in the lone house then
Stood listening in the quiet of the moonlight
  To that voice from the world of men:
Stood thronging the faint moonbeams on the dark stair,
  That goes down to the empty hall,
Hearkening in an air stirred and shaken
  By the lonely Traveller's call.
And he felt in his heart their strangeness,
  Their stillness answering his cry,

While his horse moved, cropping the dark turf,
    'Neath the starred and leafy sky;
For he suddenly smote on the door, even
    Louder, and lifted his head: –
'Tell them I came, and no one answered,
    That I kept my word,' he said.
Never the least stir made the listeners,
    Though every word he spake
Fell echoing through the shadowiness of the still house
    From the one man left awake:
Ay, they heard his foot upon the stirrup,
    And the sound of iron on stone,
And how the silence surged softly backward,
When the plunging hoofs were gone.

37

A. E. Housman
LOVELIEST OF TREES, THE CHERRY NOW

Loveliest of trees, the cherry now
Is hung with bloom along the bough,
And stands about the woodland ride
Wearing white for Eastertide.

Now, of my threescore years and ten,
Twenty will not come again,
And take from seventy springs a score,
It only leaves me fifty more.

And since to look at things in bloom
Fifty springs are little room,
About the woodlands I will go
To see the cherry hung with snow.

Marriott Edgar
THE LION AND ALBERT

There's a famous seaside place called Blackpool,
   That's noted for fresh air and fun,
And Mr and Mrs Ramsbottom
   Went there with young Albert, their son.

A grand little lad was young Albert,
   All dressed in his best; quite a swell
With a stick with an 'orse's 'ead 'andle,
   The finest that Woolworth's could sell.

They didn't think much to the Ocean:
   The waves, they was fiddlin' and small,
There was no wrecks and nobody drownded,
   Fact, nothing to laugh at at all.

So, seeking for further amusement,
   They paid and went into the Zoo,
Where they'd Lions and Tigers and Camels,
   And old ale and sandwiches too.

There were one great big Lion called Wallace;
   His nose were all covered with scars—

He lay in a somnolent posture
　　With the side of his face on the bars.

Now Albert had heard about Lions,
　　How they was ferocious and wild—
To see Wallace lying so peaceful,
　　Well, it didn't seem right to the child.

So straightway the brave little feller,
　　Not showing a morsel of fear,
Took his stick with its 'orse's 'ead 'andle
　　And poked it in Wallace's ear.

You could see that the Lion didn't like it,
　　For giving a kind of a roll,
He pulled Albert inside the cage with 'im,
　　And swallowed the little lad 'ole.

Then Pa, who had seen the occurrence,
　　And didn't know what to do next,
Said 'Mother! Yon Lion's 'et Albert,'
　　And Mother said 'Well, I am vexed!'

Then Mr and Mrs Ramsbottom—
　　Quite rightly, when all's said and done—
Complained to the Animal Keeper
　　That the Lion had eaten their son.

The keeper was quite nice about it;
　　He said 'What a nasty mishap.

Are you sure that it's *your* boy he's eaten?'
   Pa said 'Am I sure? There's his cap!'

The manager had to be sent for.
   He came and he said 'What's to do?'
Pa said 'Yon Lion's 'et Albert,
   And 'im in his Sunday clothes, too.'

Then Mother said, 'Right's right, young feller;
   I think its a shame and a sin
For a lion to go and eat Albert,
   And after we've paid to come in.'

The manager wanted no trouble,
   He took out his purse right away,
Saying 'How much to settle the matter?'
   And Pa said 'What do you usually pay?'

But Mother had turned a bit awkward
   When she thought where her Albert had gone.
She said 'No! someone's got to be summonsed'—
   So that was decided upon.

Then off they went to the P'lice Station,
   In front of the Magistrate chap;
They told 'im what happened to Albert,
   And proved it by showing his cap.

The Magistrate gave his opinion
   That no one was really to blame
And he said that he hoped the Ramsbottoms
   Would have further sons to their name.

At that Mother got proper blazing,
   'And thank you, sir, kindly,' said she.
'What, waste all our lives raising children
   To feed ruddy Lions? Not me!'

35

G. K. *Chesterton*
THE DONKEY

When fishes flew and forests walked
  And figs grew upon thorn,
Some moment when the moon was blood
  Then surely I was born.

With monstrous head and sickening cry
  And ears like errant wings,
The devil's walking parody
  On all four-footed things.

The tattered outlaw of the earth,
  Of ancient crooked will;
Starve, scourge, deride me: I am dumb,
  I keep my secret still.

Fools! For I also had my hour;
  One far fierce hour and sweet:
There was a shout about my ears,
  And palms before my feet.

34

John Keats
ODE TO A NIGHTINGALE

My heart aches, and a drowsy numbness pains
  My sense, as though of hemlock I had drunk,
Or emptied some dull opiate to the drains
  One minute past, and Lethe-wards had sunk:
'Tis not through envy of thy happy lot,
  But being too happy in thy happiness, –
    That thou, light-winged Dryad of the trees,
      In some melodious plot
  Of beechen green, and shadows numberless,
    Singest of summer in full-throated ease.

O for a draught of vintage! that hath been
  Cool'd a long age in the deep-delved earth,
Tasting of Flora and the country-green,
  Dance, and Provençal song, and sunburnt mirth!
O for a beaker full of the warm South,
  Full of the true, the blushful Hippocrene,
    With beaded bubbles winking at the brim,
      And purple-stained mouth;
  That I might drink, and leave the world unseen,
    And with thee fade away into the forest dim:

Fade far away, dissolve, and quite forget
  What thou among the leaves hast never known,
The weariness, the fever, and the fret

Here, where men sit and hear each other groan;
Where palsy shakes a few, sad, last grey hairs,
   Where youth grows pale, and spectre-thin, and dies;
      Where but to think is to be full of sorrow
            And leaden-eyed despairs;
   Where Beauty cannot keep her lustrous eyes,
      Or new Love pine at them beyond tomorrow.

Away! away! for I will fly to thee,
   Not charioted by Bacchus and his pards,
But on the viewless wings of Poesy,
   Though the dull brain perplexes and retards:
Already with thee! tender is the night,
   And haply the Queen-Moon is on her throne,
      Cluster'd around by all her starry Fays;
            But here there is no light,
   Save what from heaven is with the breezes blown
      Through verdurous glooms and winding mossy ways.

I cannot see what flowers are at my feet,
   Nor what soft incense hangs upon the boughs,
But, in embalmed darkness, guess each sweet
   Wherewith the seasonable month endows
The grass, the thicket, and the fruit-tree wild;
   White hawthorn, and the pastoral eglantine;
      Fast-fading violets cover'd up in leaves;
            And mid-May's eldest child,
   The coming musk-rose, full of dewy wine,
      The murmurous haunt of flies on summer eves.

Darkling I listen; and for many a time
  I have been half in love with easeful Death,
Call'd him soft names in many a musèd rhyme,
  To take into the air my quiet breath;
Now more than ever seems it rich to die,
  To cease upon the midnight with no pain,
    While thou art pouring forth thy soul abroad
      In such an ecstasy!
  Still wouldst thou sing, and I have ears in vain –
    To thy high requiem become a sod.

Thou wast not born for death, immortal Bird!
  No hungry generations tread thee down;
The voice I hear this passing night was heard
  In ancient days by emperor and clown:
Perhaps the self-same song that found a path
  Through the sad heart of Ruth, when, sick for home,
    She stood in tears amid the alien corn;
      The same that oft-times hath
  Charm'd magic casements, opening on the foam
  Of perilous seas, in faery lands forlorn.

Forlorn! the very word is like a bell
  To toll me back from thee to my sole self!
Adieu! the fancy cannot cheat so well
  As she is fam'd to do, deceiving elf.
Adieu! adieu! thy plaintive anthem fades
  Past the near meadows, over the still stream,
    Up the hill-side; and now 'tis buried deep
      In the next valley-glades:
  Was it a vision, or a waking dream?
    Fled is that music: – Do I wake or sleep?

33

Thomas Hood
I REMEMBER, I REMEMBER

I remember, I remember,
  The house where I was born,
The little window where the sun
  Came peeping in at morn;
He never came a wink too soon,
  Nor brought too long a day,
But now, I often wish the night
  Had borne my breath away.

I remember, I remember,
  The roses, red and white;
The violets, and the lily-cups,
  Those flowers made of light!
The lilacs where the robin built,
  And where my brother set
The laburnum on his birthday –
  The tree is living yet!

I remember, I remember,
  Where I was used to swing;
And thought the air must rush as fresh
  To swallows on the wing:
My spirit flew in feathers then,

That is so heavy now,
And summer pools could hardly cool
    The fever on my brow!

I remember, I remember,
    The fir trees dark and high;
I used to think their slender tops
    Were close against the sky:
It was a childish ignorance,
    But now 'tis little joy
To know I'm farther off from Heav'n
    Than when I was a boy.

Lord Byron
SHE WALKS IN BEAUTY

She walks in beauty, like the night
   Of cloudless climes and starry skies;
And all that's best of dark and bright
   Meet in her aspect and her eyes:
Thus mellow'd to that tender light
   Which heaven to gaudy day denies.

One shade the more, one ray the less,
   Had half impair'd the nameless grace
Which waves in every raven tress,
   Or softly lightens o'er her face;
Where thoughts serenely sweet express
   How pure, how dear their dwelling-place.

And on that cheek, and o'er that brow,
   So soft, so calm, yet eloquent,
The smiles that win, the tints that glow,
   But tell of days in goodness spent,
A mind at peace with all below,
   A heart whose love is innocent!

Oscar Wilde
(FROM) THE BALLAD OF READING GAOL

He did not wear his scarlet coat,
For blood and wine are red,
And blood and wine were on his hands
    When they found him with the dead,
The poor dead woman whom he loved,
    And murdered in her bed.

He walked amongst the Trial Men
    In a suit of shabby grey;
A cricket cap was on his head,
    And his step seemed light and gay;
But I never saw a man who looked
    So wistfully at the day.

I never saw a man who looked
    With such a wistful eye
Upon that little tent of blue
    Which prisoners call the sky,
And at every drifting cloud that went
    With sails of silver by.

I walked, with other souls in pain,
    Within another ring,

And was wondering if the man had done
　　　　A great or little thing,
When a voice behind me whispered low,
　　　　That fellow's got to swing!

Six weeks our guardsman walked the yard,
　　　　In the suit of shabby grey:
His cricket cap was on his head,
　　　　And his step seemed light and gay,
But I never saw a man who looked
　　　　So wistfully at the day.

I never saw a man who looked
　　　　With such a wistful eye
Upon that little tent of blue
　　　　Which prisoners call the sky,
And at every wandering cloud that trailed
　　　　Its ravelled fleeces by.

He did not wring his hands, as do
　　　　Those witless men who dare
To try to rear the changeling Hope
　　　　In the cave of black Despair:
He only looked upon the sun,
　　　　And drank the morning air.

He did not wring his hands nor weep,
　　　　Nor did he peek or pine,
But he drank the air as though it held
　　　　Some healthful anodyne;

With open mouth he drank the sun
     As though it had been wine!

And I and all the souls in pain,
     Who tramped the other ring,
Forgot if we ourselves had done
     A great or little thing,
And watched with gaze of dull amaze
     The man who had to swing.

And strange it was to see him pass
     With a step so light and gay,
And strange it was to see him look
     So wistfully at the day,
And strange it was to think that he
     Had such a debt to pay.

30

Edward Thomas
ADLESTROP

Yes. I remember Adlestrop –
The name, because one afternoon
Of heat the express-train drew up there
Unwontedly. It was late June.

The steam hissed. Some one cleared his throat.
No one left and no one came
On the bare platform. What I saw
Was Adlestrop – only the name

And willows, willow-herb, and grass,
And meadowsweet, and haycocks dry,
No whit less still and lonely fair
Than the high cloudlets in the sky.

And for that minute a blackbird sang
Close by, and around him, mistier,
Farther and farther, all the birds
Of Oxfordshire and Gloucestershire.

29

Andrew Marvell
TO HIS COY MISTRESS

Had we but world enough, and time,
This coyness, Lady, were no crime.
We would sit down, and think which way
To walk, and pass our long love's day.
Thou by the Indian Ganges' side
Shouldst rubies find: I by the tide
Of Humber would complain. I would
Love you ten years before the Flood,
And you should, if you please, refuse
Till the conversion of the Jews.
My vegetable love should grow
Vaster than empires, and more slow.
An hundred years should go to praise
Thine eyes, and on thy forehead gaze;
Two hundred to adore each breast,
But thirty thousand to the rest.
An age at least to every part,
And the last age should show your heart.
For, Lady, you deserve this state,
Nor would I love at lower rate.
    But at my back I always hear
Time's wingèd chariot hurrying near;
And yonder all before us lie

Deserts of vast eternity.
Thy beauty shall no more be found,
Nor, in my marble vault, shall sound
My echoing song: then worms shall try
That long preserved virginity,
And your quaint honour turn to dust,
And into ashes all my lust.
The grave's a fine and private place,
But none, I think, do there embrace.
  Now, therefore, while the youthful hue
Sits on thy skin like morning dew,
And while thy willing soul transpires
At every pore with instant fires,
Now let us sport us while we may,
And now, like amorous birds of prey,
Rather at once our time devour,
Than languish in his slow-chapt power.
Let us roll all our strength, and all
Our sweetness, up into one ball,
And tear our pleasures with rough strife
Thorough the iron gates of life:
Thus, though we cannot make our sun
Stand still, yet we will make him run.

28

Samuel Taylor Coleridge

THE RIME OF THE ANCIENT MARINER

PART I
It is an ancient Mariner,
And he stoppeth one of three.
'By thy long grey beard and glittering eye,
Now wherefore stopp'st thou me?

The Bridegroom's doors are opened wide,
And I am next of kin;
The guests are met, the feast is set:
May'st hear the merry din.'

He holds him with his skinny hand,
'There was a ship,' quoth he.
'Hold off: unhand me, greybeard loon!'
Eftsoons his hand dropt he.

He holds him with his glittering eye –
The Wedding-Guest stood still,
And listens like a three years' child:
The Mariner hath his will.

The Wedding-Guest sat on a stone:
He cannot choose but hear;

And thus spake on that ancient man,
The bright-eyed Mariner.

'The ship was cheered, the harbour cleared,
Merrily did we drop
Below the kirk, below the hill,
Below the lighthouse top.

The Sun came up upon the left,
Out of the sea came he!
And he shone bright, and on the right
Went down into the sea.

Higher and higher every day,
Till over the mast at noon –'
The Wedding-Guest here beat his breast,
For he heard the loud bassoon.

The bride hath paced into the hall,
Red as a rose is she;
Nodding their heads before her goes
The merry minstrelsy.

The Wedding-Guest he beat his breast,
Yet he cannot choose but hear;
And thus spake on that ancient man,
The bright-eyed Mariner.

'And now the Storm-blast came, and he
Was tyrannous and strong:

He struck with his o'ertaking wings,
And chased us south along.

With sloping masts and dipping prow,
As who pursued with yell and blow
Still treads the shadow of his foe,
And forward bends his head,
The ship drove fast, loud roared the blast,
And southward aye we fled.

And now there came both mist and snow,
And it grew wondrous cold:
And ice, mast-high, came floating by,
As green as emerald.

And through the drifts the snowy clifts
Did send a dismal sheen:
Nor shapes of men nor beasts we ken –
The ice was all between.

The ice was here, the ice was there,
The ice was all around:
It cracked and growled, and roared and howled,
Like noises in a swound!

At length did cross an Albatross,
Thorough the fog it came;
As if it had been a Christian soul,
We hailed it in God's name.

It ate the food it ne'er had eat,
And round and round it flew.
The ice did split with a thunder-fit;
The helmsman steered us through!

And a good south wind sprung up behind;
The Albatross did follow,
And every day, for food or play,
Came to the mariner's hollo!

In mist or cloud, on mast or shroud,
It perched for vespers nine;
Whiles all the night, through fog-smoke white,
Glimmered the white Moon-shine.'

'God save thee, ancient Mariner!
From the fiends, that plague thee thus! –
Why look'st thou so?' – 'With my cross-bow
I shot the Albatross!'

Rupert Brooke
(FROM) THE OLD VICARAGE, GRANTCHESTER
(Café des Westens, Berlin, May 1912)

Just now the lilac is in bloom,
All before my little room;
And in my flower-beds, I think,
Smile the carnation and the pink;
And down the borders, well I know,
The poppy and the pansy blow ...
Oh! there the chestnuts, summer through,
Beside the river make for you
A tunnel of green gloom, and sleep
Deeply above; and green and deep
The stream mysterious glides beneath,
Green as a dream and deep as death.
– Oh, damn! I know it! and I know
How the May fields all golden show,
And when the day is young and sweet,
Gild gloriously the bare feet.
That run to bathe ...

                                        Du lieber Gott!

Here am I, sweating, sick, and hot,
And there the shadowed waters fresh
Lean up to embrace the naked flesh.

Temperamentvoll German Jews
Drink beer around; – and *there* the dews
Are soft beneath a morn of gold.
Here tulips bloom as they are told;
Unkempt about those hedges blows
An English unofficial rose;
And there the unregulated sun
Slopes down to rest when day is done,
And wakes a vague unpunctual star,
A slippered Hesper; and there are
Meads towards Haslingfield and Coton
Where *das Betreten*'s not *verboten*.

Ειυε γεψοιμηψ . . . would I were
In Grantchester, in Grantchester! –
Some, it may be, can get in touch
With Nature there, or Earth, or such.
And clever modern men have seen
A Faun a-peeping through the green,
And felt the Classics were not dead,
To glimpse a Naiad's reedy head,
Or hear the Goat-foot piping low: . . .
But these are things I do not know.
I only know that you may lie
Day-long and watch the Cambridge sky,
And, flower-lulled in sleepy grass,
Hear the cool lapse of hours pass.
Until the centuries blend and blur
In Grantchester, in Grantchester –
Still in the dawnlit waters cool

162

His ghostly Lordship swims his pool,
And tries the strokes, essays the tricks,
Long learnt on Hellespont, or Styx.
Dan Chaucer hears his river still
Chatter beneath a phantom mill.
Tennyson notes, with studious eye,
How Cambridge waters hurry by . . .
And in that garden, black and white,
Creep whispers through the grass all night;
And spectral dance, before the dawn,
A hundred Vicars down the lawn;
Curates, long dust, will come and go
On lissom, clerical, printless toe;
And oft between the boughs is seen
The sly shade of a Rural Dean . . .
Till, at a shiver in the skies,
Vanishing with Satanic cries,
The prim ecclesiastic rout
Leaves but a startled sleeper-out,
Grey heavens, the first bird's drowsy calls,
The falling house that never falls.

God! I will pack, and take a train,
And get me to England once again!
For England's the one land, I know,
Where men with Splendid Hearts may go;
And Cambridgeshire, of all England,
The shire for Men who Understand;
And of *that* district I prefer
The lovely hamlet Grantchester.

For Cambridge people rarely smile,
Being urban, squat, and packed with guile . . .

   Ah God! to see the branches stir
Across the moon at Grantchester!
To smell the thrilling-sweet and rotten
Unforgettable, unforgotten
River-smell, and hear the breeze
Sobbing in the little trees.
Say, do the elm-clumps greatly stand
Still guardians of that holy land?
The chestnuts shade, in reverend dream,
The yet unacademic stream?
Is dawn a secret shy and cold
Anadyomene, silver-gold?
And sunset still a golden sea
From Haslingfield to Madingley?
And after, ere the night is born,
Do hares come out about the corn?
Oh, is the water sweet and cool,
Gentle and brown, above the pool?
And laughs the immortal river still
Under the mill, under the mill?
Say, is there Beauty yet to find?
And Certainty and Quiet kind?
Deep meadows yet, for to forget
The lies, and truths, and pain? . . . Oh! yet
Stands the Church clock at ten to three?
And is there honey still for tea?

26

Sir John Betjeman
DIARY OF A CHURCH MOUSE

Here among long-discarded cassocks,
Damp stools, and half-split open hassocks,
Here where the Vicar never looks
I nibble through old service books.
Lean and alone I spend my days
Behind this Church of England baize.
I share my dark forgotten room
With two oil-lamps and half a broom.
The cleaner never bothers me,
So here I eat my frugal tea.
My bread is sawdust mixed with straw;
My jam is polish for the floor.
  Christmas and Easter may be feasts
For congregations and for priests,
And so may Whitsun. All the same,
They do not fill my meagre frame.
For me the only feast at all
Is Autumn's Harvest Festival,
When I can satisfy my want
With ears of corn around the font.
I climb the eagle's brazen head
To burrow through a loaf of bread.
I scramble up the pulpit stair

And gnaw the marrows hanging there.
   It is enjoyable to taste
These items ere they go to waste,
But how annoying when one finds
That other mice with pagan minds
Come into church my food to share
Who have no proper business there.
Two field mice who have no desire
To be baptized, invade the choir.
A large and most unfriendly rat
Comes in to see what we are at.
He says he thinks there is no God
And yet he comes . . . it's rather odd.
This year he stole a sheaf of wheat
(It screened our special preacher's seat),
And prosperous mice from fields away
Come in to hear the organ play,
And under cover of its notes
Ate through the altar's sheaf of oats.
A Low Church mouse, who thinks that I
Am too papistical, and High,
Yet somehow doesn't think it wrong
To munch through Harvest Evensong,
While I, who starve the whole year through,
Must share my food with rodents who
Except at this time of the year
Not once inside the church appear.
   Within the human world I know
Such goings-on could not be so,
For human beings only do
What their religion tells them to.

They read the Bible every day
And always, night and morning, pray,
And just like me, the good church mouse,
Worship each week in God's own house,
    But all the same it's strange to me
How very full the church can be
With people I don't see at all
Except at Harvest Festival.

25

W. B. Yeats
WHEN YOU ARE OLD

When you are old and grey and full of sleep,
And nodding by the fire, take down this book,
And slowly read, and dream of the soft look
Your eyes had once, and of their shadows deep;

How many loved your moments of glad grace,
And loved your beauty with love false or true,
But one man loved the pilgrim soul in you,
And loved the sorrows of your changing face;

And bending down beside the glowing bars,
Murmur, a little sadly, how Love fled
And paced upon the mountains overhead
And hid his face amid a crowd of stars.

24

W. H. Auden
FUNERAL BLUES (STOP ALL THE CLOCKS)

Stop all the clocks, cut off the telephone,
Prevent the dog from barking with a juicy bone,
Silence the pianos and with muffled drum
Bring out the coffin, let the mourners come.

Let aeroplanes circle moaning overhead
Scribbling on the sky the message He Is Dead,
Put crepe bows round the white necks of the public doves,
Let the traffic policemen wear black cotton gloves.

He was my North, my South, my East and West,
My working week and my Sunday rest,
My noon, my midnight, my talk, my song;
I thought that love would last for ever: I was wrong.

The stars are not wanted now: put out every one;
Pack up the moon and dismantle the sun;
Pour away the ocean and sweep up the wood.
For nothing now can ever come to any good.

T. S. Eliot

MACAVITY: THE MYSTERY CAT

Macavity's a Mystery Cat: he's called the Hidden Paw –
For he's the master criminal who can defy the Law.
He's the bafflement of Scotland Yard, the Flying Squad's despair:
For when they reach the scene of crime – *Macavity's not there!*

Macavity, Macavity, there's no one like Macavity,
He's broken every human law, he breaks the law of gravity.
His powers of levitation would make a fakir stare,
And when you reach the scene of crime – *Macavity's not there!*
You may seek him in the basement, you may look up in the air –
But I tell you once and once again, *Macavity's not there!*

Macavity's a ginger cat, he's very tall and thin;
You would know him if you saw him, for his eyes are sunken in.
His brow is deeply lined with thought, his head is highly domed;
His coat is dusty from neglect, his whiskers are uncombed.
He sways his head from side to side, with movements like a snake;
And when you think he's half asleep, he's always wide awake.

Macavity, Macavity, there's no one like Macavity,
For he's a fiend in feline shape, a monster of depravity.
You may meet him in a by-street, you may see him in the square –
But when a crime's discovered, then *Macavity's not there!*

He's outwardly respectable. (They say he cheats at cards.)
And his footprints are not found in any file of Scotland Yard's.
And when the larder's looted, or the jewel-case is rifled,
Or when the milk is missing, or another Peke's been stifled,
Or the greenhouse glass is broken, and the trellis past repair –
Ay, there's the wonder of the thing! *Macavity's not there*!

And when the Foreign Office find a Treaty's gone astray,
Or the Admiralty lose some plans and drawings by the way,
There may be a scrap of paper in the hall or on the stair –
But it's useless to investigate – *Macavity's not there*!
And when the loss has been disclosed, the Secret Service say:
'It *must* have been Macavity!' – but he's a mile away.
You'll be sure to find him resting, or a-licking of his thumbs,
Or engaged in doing complicated long division sums.

Macavity, Macavity, there's no one like Macavity,
There never was a Cat of such deceitfulness and suavity.
He always has an alibi, and one or two to spare:
At whatever time the deed took place – MACAVITY WASN'T THERE!
And they say that all the Cats whose wicked deeds are widely
    known
(I might mention Mungojerrie, I might mention Griddlebone)
Are nothing more than agents for the Cat who all the time
Just controls their operations: the Napoleon of Crime!

22

Gerard Manley Hopkins
PIED BEAUTY

Glory be to God for dappled things –
    For skies of couple-colour as a brinded cow;
      For rose-moles all in stipple upon trout that swim;
Fresh-firecoal chestnut-falls; finches' wings;
    Landscape plotted and pieced – fold, fallow, and plough;
      And all trades, their gear and tackle and trim.

All things counter, original, spare, strange;
    Whatever is fickle, freckled (who knows how?)
        With swift, slow; sweet, sour; adazzle, dim;
He fathers-forth whose beauty is past change:
          Praise him.

21

Robert Browning
HOME-THOUGHTS FROM ABROAD

Oh, to be in England
Now that April's there,
And whoever wakes in England
Sees, some morning, unaware,
That the lowest boughs and the brushwood sheaf
Round the elm-tree bole are in tiny leaf,
While the chaffinch sings on the orchard bough
In England – now!

And after April, when May follows,
And the whitethroat builds, and all the swallows –
Hark! where my blossomed pear-tree in the hedge
Leans to the field and scatters on the clover
Blossoms and dewdrops – at the bent spray's edge –
That's the wise thrush; he sings each song twice over,
Lest you should think he never could recapture
The first fine careless rapture!
And though the fields look rough with hoary dew,
All will be gay when noontide wakes anew
The buttercups, the little children's dower,
– Far brighter than this gaudy melon-flower!

Edward Lear

THE OWL AND THE PUSSYCAT

The Owl and the Pussy-Cat went to sea
    In a beautiful pea-green boat,
They took some honey, and plenty of money
    Wrapped up in a five-pound note.
The Owl looked up to the stars above,
    And sang to a small guitar,
'O lovely Pussy! O Pussy, my love,
What a beautiful Pussy you are
        You are,
        You are!
What a beautiful Pussy you are!'

Pussy said to Owl, 'You elegant fowl!
    How charmingly sweet you sing!
O let us be married! too long we have tarried
    But what shall we do for a ring?'
They sailed away, for a year and a day,
    To the land where the Bong-Tree grows,
And there in a wood a Piggy-wig stood,
With a ring at the end of his nose,
        His nose,
        His nose!
With a ring at the end of his nose.

'Dear Pig, are you willing to sell for one shilling
    Your ring?' Said the Piggy, 'I will.'
So they took it away, and were married next day
    By the Turkey who lives on the hill.
They dinèd on mince, and slices of quince,
    Which they ate with a runcible spoon;
And hand in hand, on the edge of the sand
    They danced by the light of the moon,
        The moon,
        The moon,
They danced by the light of the moon.

19

W. B. Yeats
THE LAKE ISLE OF INNISFREE

I will arise and go now, and go to Innisfree,
And a small cabin build there, of clay and wattles made:
Nine bean-rows will I have there, a hive for the honey-bee,
And live alone in the bee-loud glade.

And I shall have some peace there, for peace comes dropping
    slow,
Dropping from the veils of the morning to where the cricket
    sings;
There midnight's all a glimmer, and noon a purple glow,
And evening full of the linnet's wings.

I will arise and go now, for always night and day
I hear lake water lapping with low sounds by the shore;
While I stand on the roadway, or on the pavements grey,
I hear it in the deep heart's core.

18

Samuel Taylor Coleridge
KUBLA KHAN

In Xanadu did Kubla Khan
A stately pleasure-dome decree:
Where Alph, the sacred river, ran
Through caverns measureless to man
   Down to a sunless sea.
So twice five miles of fertile ground
With walls and towers were girdled round:
And there were gardens bright with sinuous rills,
Where blossomed many an incense-bearing tree;
And here were forests ancient as the hills,
Enfolding sunny spots of greenery.

But oh! that deep romantic chasm which slanted
Down the green hill athwart a cedarn cover!
A savage place! as holy and enchanted
As e'er beneath a waning moon was haunted
By woman wailing for her demon-lover!
And from this chasm, with ceaseless turmoil seething,
As if this earth in fast thick pants were breathing,
A mighty fountain momently was forced:
Amid whose swift half-intermitted burst
Huge fragments vaulted like rebounding hail,

Or chaffy grain beneath the thresher's flail:
And 'mid these dancing rocks at once and ever
It flung up momently the sacred river.
Five miles meandering with a mazy motion
Through wood and dale the sacred river ran,
Then reached the caverns measureless to man,
And sank in tumult to a lifeless ocean:
And 'mid this tumult Kubla heard from far
Ancestral voices prophesying war!

   The shadow of the dome of pleasure
   Floated midway on the waves;
   Where was heard the mingled measure
   From the fountain and the caves.
It was a miracle of rare device,
A sunny pleasure-dome with caves of ice!

   A damsel with a dulcimer
   In a vision once I saw:
   It was an Abyssinian maid,
   And on her dulcimer she played,
   Singing of Mount Abora.
   Could I revive within me
   Her symphony and song,
   To such a deep delight 'twould win me,
That with music loud and long,
I would build that dome in air,
That sunny dome! those caves of ice!
And all who heard should see them there,
And all should cry, 'Beware! Beware!

His flashing eyes, his floating hair!
Weave a circle round him thrice,
And close your eyes with holy dread,
For he on honey-dew hath fed,
And drunk the milk of Paradise.'

17

Lewis Carroll
JABBERWOCKY

'Twas brillig, and the slithy toves
   Did gyre and gimble in the wabe;
All mimsy were the borogroves,
   And the mome raths outgrabe.

'Beware the Jabberwock, my son!
   The jaws that bite, the claws that catch!
Beware the Jubjub bird, and shun
   The frumious Bandersnatch!'

He took his vorpal sword in hand:
   Long time the manxome foe he sought –
So rested he by the Tumtum tree,
   And stood awhile in thought.

And as in uffish thought he stood,
   The Jabberwock, with eyes of flame,
Came whiffling through the tulgey wood,
   And burbled as it came!

One, two! One, two! And through and through
   The vorpal blade went snicker-snack!

He left it dead, and with its head
   He went galumphing back.

'And thou hast slain the Jabberwock?
   Come to my arms, my beamish boy!
O frabjous day! Callooh! Callay!'
   He chortled in his joy.

'Twas brillig, and the slithy toves
   Did gyre and gimble in the wabe;
All mimsy were the borogroves,
   And the mome raths outgrabe.

16

William Shakespeare
SONNET 116 – 'LET ME NOT TO THE
MARRIAGE . . . '

Let me not to the marriage of true minds
Admit impediments. Love is not love
Which alters when it alteration finds,
Or bends with the remover to remove:
O no! it is an ever-fixed mark,
That looks on tempests and is never shaken;
It is the star to every wandering bark,
Whose worth's unknown, although his height be taken.
Love's not Time's fool, though rosy lips and cheeks
Within his bending sickle's compass come;
Love alters not with his brief hours and weeks,
But bears it out even to the edge of doom:
　　　　If this be error and upon me proved,
　　　　I never writ, nor no man ever loved.

15

Wilfred Owen
ANTHEM FOR DOOMED YOUTH

What passing-bells for these who die as cattle?
  Only the monstrous anger of the guns.
  Only the stuttering rifles' rapid rattle
Can patter out their hasty orisons.
No mockeries now for them; no prayers nor bells,
  Nor any voice of mourning save the choirs, –
The shrill, demented choirs of wailing shells;
  And bugles calling for them from sad shires.

What candles may be held to speed them all?
  Not in the hands of boys, but in their eyes
Shall shine the holy glimmers of good-byes.
  The pallor of girls' brows shall be their pall;
Their flowers the tenderness of patient minds,
And each slow dusk a drawing-down of blinds.

14

William Blake
THE TYGER

Tyger! Tyger! burning bright
In the forests of the night,
What immortal hand or eye
Could frame thy fearful symmetry?

In what distant deeps or skies
Burnt the fire of thine eyes?
On what wings dare he aspire?
What the hand dare seize the fire?

And what shoulder, & what art,
Could twist the sinews of thy heart?
And when thy heart began to beat,
What dread hand? & what dread feet?

What the hammer? what the chain?
In what furnace was thy brain?
What the anvil? what dread grasp
Dare its deadly terrors clasp?

When the stars threw down their spears,
And water'd heaven with their tears,

Did he smile his work to see?
Did he who made the Lamb make thee?

Tyger! Tyger! burning bright
In the forests of the night,
What immortal hand or eye,
Dare frame thy fearful symmetry?

13

Percy Bysshe Shelley
OZYMANDIAS OF EGYPT

I met a traveller from an antique land
Who said: Two vast and trunkless legs of stone
Stand in the desert . . . Near them, on the sand,
Half sunk, a shattered visage lies, whose frown,
And wrinkled lip, and sneer of cold command,
Tell that its sculptor well those passions read
Which yet survive, stamped on these lifeless things,
The hand that mocked them, and the heart that fed;
And on the pedestal these words appear:
'My name is Ozymandias, king of kings:
Look on my works, ye Mighty, and despair!'
Nothing beside remains. Round the decay
Of that colossal wreck, boundless and bare,
The lone and level sands stretch far away.

12

William Wordsworth
UPON WESTMINSTER BRIDGE

Sept. 3, 1802

Earth has not anything to show more fair:
Dull would he be of soul who could pass by
A sight so touching in its majesty:
This City now doth like a garment wear

The beauty of the morning: silent, bare,
Ships, towers, domes, theatres, and temples lie
Open unto the fields, and to the sky,
All bright and glittering in the smokeless air.

Never did sun more beautifully steep
In his first splendour valley, rock, or hill;
Ne'er saw I, never felt, a calm so deep!

The river glideth at his own sweet will:
Dear God! the very houses seem asleep;
And all that mighty heart is lying still!

11

Thomas Gray
(FROM) ELEGY WRITTEN IN A COUNTRY
CHURCHYARD

The curfew tolls the Knell of parting Day,
   The lowing Herd wind slowly o'er the Lea,
The Plow-man homeward plods his weary Way,
   And leaves the World to Darkness, and to me.
Now fades the glimmering Landscape on the Sight,
   And all the Air a solemn Stillness holds;
Save where the Beetle wheels his droning Flight,
   And drowsy Tinklings lull the distant Folds.
Save that from yonder Ivy-mantled Tow'r
   The mopeing Owl does to the Moon complain
Of such as, wand'ring near her secret Bow'r,
   Molest her ancient solitary Reign.
Beneath whose rugged Elms, that Yew-Tree's Shade,
   Where heaves the Turf in many a mould'ring Heap,
Each in his narrow Cell for ever laid,
   The rude Forefathers of the Hamlet sleep.
The breezy Call of Incense-breathing Morn,
   The Swallow twitt'ring from the Straw-built Shed,
The Cock's shrill Clarion, or the echoing Horn,
   No more shall rouse them from their lowly Bed.
For them no more the blazing Hearth shall burn,
   Or busy Housewife ply her Evening Care:
No Children run to lisp their Sire's Return,

Or climb his Knees the envied Kiss to share.
Oft did the Harvest to their Sickle yield,
    Their Furrow oft the stubborn Glebe has broke;
How jocund did they drive their Team afield!
    How bow'd the Woods beneath their sturdy Stroke!
Let not Ambition mock their useful Toil,
    Their homely Joys and Destiny obscure;
Nor Grandeur hear with a disdainful Smile,
    The short and simple Annals of the Poor.

Elizabeth Barrett Browning
HOW DO I LOVE THEE?
(from Sonnets from the Portuguese)

XLIII
How do I love thee? Let me count the ways.
I love thee to the depth and breadth and height
My soul can reach, when feeling out of sight
For the ends of Being and ideal Grace.
I love thee to the level of everyday's
Most quiet need, by sun and candlelight.
I love thee freely, as men strive for Right;
I love thee purely, as they turn from Praise.
I love thee with the passion put to use
In my old griefs, and with my childhood's faith.
I love thee with a love I seemed to lose
With my lost saints, – I love thee with the breath,
Smiles, tears, of all my life! – and, if God choose,
I shall but love thee better after death.

9

Wilfred Owen
DULCE ET DECORUM EST

Bent double, like old beggars under sacks,
Knock-kneed, coughing like hags, we cursed through sludge,
Till on the haunting flares we turned our backs
And towards our distant rest began to trudge.
Men marched asleep. Many had lost their boots
But limped on, blood-shod. All went lame; all blind;
Drunk with fatigue; deaf even to the hoots
Of tired, outstripped Five-Nines that dropped behind.

Gas! Gas! Quick, boys! – An ecstasy of fumbling,
Fitting the clumsy helmets just in time;
But someone still was yelling out and stumbling
And flound'ring like a man in fire or lime . . .
Dim, through the misty panes and thick green light,
As under a green sea, I saw him drowning.

In all my dreams, before my helpless sight,
He plunges at me, guttering, choking, drowning.

If in some smothering dreams you too could pace
Behind the wagon that we flung him in,
And watch the white eyes writhing in his face,
His hanging face, like a devil's sick of sin;

If you could hear, at every jolt, the blood
Come gargling from the froth-corrupted lungs,
Obscene as cancer, bitter as the cud
Of vile, incurable sores on innocent tongues, –
My friend, you would not tell with such high zest
To children ardent for some desperate glory,
The old Lie: Dulce et decorum est
Pro patria mori.

8

W. B. Yeats
HE WISHES FOR THE CLOTHS OF HEAVEN

Had I the heavens' embroidered cloths,
Enwrought with golden and silver light,
The blue and the dim and the dark cloths
Of night and light and the half-light,
I would spread the cloths under your feet:
But I, being poor, have only my dreams;
I have spread my dreams under your feet;
Tread softly because you tread on my dreams.

7

Alfred, Lord Tennyson
THE LADY OF SHALOTT

PART I
On either side the river lie
Long fields of barley and of rye,
That clothe the wold and meet the sky;
And thro' the field the road runs by
        To many-tower'd Camelot;
And up and down the people go,
Gazing where the lilies blow
Round an island there below,
        The island of Shalott.

Willows whiten, aspens quiver,
Little breezes dusk and shiver
Thro' the wave that runs for ever
By the island in the river
        Flowing down to Camelot.
Four grey walls, and four grey towers,
Overlook a space of flowers,
And the silent isle imbowers
        The Lady of Shalott.

By the margin, willow-veil'd,
Slide the heavy barges trail'd

By slow horses; and unhail'd
The shallop flitteth silken-sail'd
   Skimming down to Camelot:
But who hath seen her wave her hand?
Or at the casement seen her stand?
Or is she known in all the land,
   The Lady of Shalott?

Only reapers, reaping early
In among the bearded barley,
Hear a song that echoes cheerly
From the river winding clearly,
   Down to tower'd Camelot:
And by the moon the reaper weary
Piling sheaves in uplands airy,
Listening, whispers, ''Tis the fairy
   Lady of Shalott.'

6

William Shakespeare
SONNET 18 — 'SHALL I COMPARE THEE . . .'

Shall I compare thee to a summer's day?
Thou art more lovely and more temperate:
Rough winds do shake the darling buds of May,
And summer's lease hath all too short a date:
Sometime too hot the eye of heaven shines,
And often is his gold complexion dimm'd;
And every fair from fair sometime declines,
By chance, or nature's changing course, untrimm'd;
But thy eternal summer shall not fade
Nor lose possession of that fair thou ow'st,
Nor shall Death brag thou wand'rest in his shade
When in eternal lines to time thou grow'st:
   So long as men can breathe or eyes can see,
   So long lives this, and this gives life to thee.

5

Rupert Brooke
THE SOLDIER

If I should die, think only this of me:
  That there's some corner of a foreign field
That is for ever England. There shall be
  In that rich earth a richer dust concealed;
A dust whom England bore, shaped, made aware,
  Gave, once, her flowers to love, her ways to roam,
A body of England's, breathing English air,
  Washed by the rivers, blest by suns of home.

And think, this heart, all evil shed away,
  A pulse in the eternal mind, no less
    Gives somewhere back the thoughts by England given;
Her sights and sounds; dreams happy as her day;
  And laughter, learnt of friends; and gentleness,
    In hearts at peace, under an English heaven.

4

John Keats
TO AUTUMN

Season of mists and mellow fruitfulness,
 Close bosom-friend of the maturing sun;
Conspiring with him how to load and bless
 With fruit the vines that round the thatch-eaves run;
To bend with apples the moss'd cottage-trees,
 And fill all fruit with ripeness to the core;
 To swell the gourd, and plump the hazel shells
With a sweet kernel; to set budding more,
 And still more, later flowers for the bees,
 Until they think warm days will never cease,
 For Summer has o'er-brimm'd their clammy cells.

Who hath not seen thee oft amid thy store?
 Sometimes whoever seeks abroad may find
Thee sitting careless on a granary floor,
 Thy hair soft-lifted by the winnowing wind;
Or on a half-reap'd furrow sound asleep,
 Drows'd with the fume of poppies, while thy hook
 Spares the next swath and all its twined flowers:
And sometimes like a gleaner thou dost keep
 Steady thy laden head across a brook;
 Or by a cider-press, with patient look,
 Thou watchest the last oozings, hours by hours.

Where are the songs of Spring? Ay, where are they?
  Think not of them, thou hast thy music too, –
While barred clouds bloom the soft-dying day,
  And touch the stubble-plains with rosy hue;
Then in a wailful choir the small gnats mourn
    Among the river sallows, borne aloft
      Or sinking as the light wind lives or dies;
And full-grown lambs loud bleat from hilly bourn;
  Hedge-crickets sing; and now with treble soft
The red-breast whistles from a garden croft;
    And gathering swallows twitter in the skies.

3

Jenny Joseph
WARNING

When I am an old woman I shall wear purple
With a red hat which doesn't go, and doesn't suit me.
And I shall spend my pension on brandy and summer gloves
And satin sandals, and say we've no money for butter.
I shall sit down on the pavement when I'm tired
And gobble up samples in shops and press alarm bells
And run my stick along the public railings
And make up for the sobriety of my youth.
I shall go out in my slippers in the rain
And pick the flowers in other people's gardens
And learn to spit.

You can wear terrible shirts and grow more fat
And eat three pounds of sausages at a go
Or only bread and pickle for a week
And hoard pens and pencils and beermats and things in boxes.

But now we must have clothes that keep us dry
And pay our rent and not swear in the street
And set a good example for the children.
We must have friends to dinner and read the papers.

But maybe I ought to practise a little now?
So people who know me are not too shocked and surprised
When suddenly I am old, and start to wear purple.

William Wordsworth
THE DAFFODILS

I wander'd lonely as a cloud
That floats on high o'er vales and hills,
When all at once I saw a crowd,
A host of golden daffodils,
Beside the lake, beneath the trees
Fluttering and dancing in the breeze.

Continuous as the stars that shine
And twinkle on the milky way,
They stretch'd in never-ending line
Along the margin of a bay:
Ten thousand saw I at a glance
Tossing their heads in sprightly dance.

The waves beside them danced, but they
Out-did the sparkling waves in glee: –
A Poet could not but be gay
In such a jocund company!
I gazed – and gazed – but little thought
What wealth the show to me had brought.

For oft, when on my couch I lie
In vacant or in pensive mood,

They flash upon that inward eye
Which is the bliss of solitude;
And then my heart with pleasure fills,
And dances with the daffodils.

1

Rudyard Kipling
I F
('Brother Square-Toes' – *Rewards and Fairies*)

If you can keep your head when all about you
    Are losing theirs and blaming it on you,
If you can trust yourself when all men doubt you,
    But make allowance for their doubting too;
If you can wait and not be tired by waiting,
    Or being lied about, don't deal in lies,
Or being hated, don't give way to hating,
    And yet don't look too good, nor talk too wise:

If you can dream – and not make dreams your master;
    If you can think – and not make thoughts your aim;
If you can meet with Triumph and Disaster
    And treat those two impostors just the same;
If you can bear to hear the truth you've spoken
    Twisted by knaves to make a trap for fools,
Or watch the things you gave your life to, broken,
    And stoop and build 'em up with worn-out tools:

If you can make one heap of all your winnings
    And risk it on one turn of pitch-and-toss,
And lose, and start again at your beginnings
    And never breathe a word about your loss;
If you can force your heart and nerve and sinew

To serve your turn long after they are gone,
And so hold on when there is nothing in you
    Except the Will which says to them: 'Hold on!'

If you can talk with crowds and keep your virtue,
    Or walk with Kings – nor lose the common touch,
If neither foes nor loving friends can hurt you,
    If all men count with you, but none too much;
If you can fill the unforgiving minute
    With sixty seconds' worth of distance run,
Yours is the Earth and everything that's in it,
    And – which is more – you'll be a Man, my son!

POEMS FOR OCCASIONS

I've often been asked to suggest poems to be read aloud at special occasions – sadly it's usually funerals – or sometimes, 'Do you know any really good patriotic poems?' It's obvious that poetry can express emotions in a way that we find comforting or inspiring. So, here are poems that celebrate different topics or emotions. All the poems are to be found in this book. It's very much a personal choice, so readers may well know or discover other poems that are more suitable – and you may want to make your own selections for other events.

LOVE
The Passionate Shepherd To His Love – Christopher Marlowe
The Good-Morrow – John Donne
She Walks In Beauty – Lord Byron
To His Coy Mistress – Andrew Marvell
When You Are Old – W. B. Yeats
Sonnet 116 –'Let me not to the marriage . . . ' – William
    Shakespeare
How Do I Love Thee – Elizabeth Barrett Browning
He Wishes For The Cloths Of Heaven – W. B. Yeats
Sonnet 18 – 'Shall I Compare thee . . . ' – William Shakespeare
Greensleeves – Anon
Love – George Herbert

AUTUMN
Ode To Autumn – John Keats

WINTER
Journey Of The Magi – T. S. Eliot
The Darkling Thrush – Thomas Hardy

ACKNOWLEDGEMENTS

The publisher wishes to thank the following for permission to reproduce the following copyright material, as listed below:

Allan Ahlberg: 'Please Mrs Butler' from *Please Mrs Butler* (Kestrel Books, 1983), copyright © Allan Ahlberg, 1983, reproduced by permission of Penguin Books Ltd.

W. H. Auden: 'Stop All The Clocks' and 'Night Mail' from *Collected Shorter Poems 1927-1957* (Faber & Faber, 1969), copyright © 1940 by W. H. Auden and 1938 by W. H. Auden, reproduced by permission of Faber & Faber Ltd. and Curtis Brown Ltd.

John Betjeman: 'Diary of a Church Mouse' from *John Betjeman's Collected Poems* (John Murray, 1972), reproduced by permission of John Murray (Publishers) Ltd.

Noël Coward: 'Mad Dogs and Englishmen' from *Words and Review* (1932), reproduced by permission of A & C Black Publishers and Alan Brodie Representation on behalf of NC Aventales AG.

W. H. Davies: 'Leisure' from *The Complete Poems of W.H. Davies* (Jonathan Cape, 1967), reproduced by permission of Dee & Griffin on behalf of Mrs H. M. Davies Trust.

INDEX OF POEMS BY TITLE

INDEX OF FIRST LINES

INDEX OF POETS